Never

DULL!

Debbie
God Bless
Heather Sharp

Heather Sharp

The black and white photos in this book do not do justice to Dad's blond wig and red hat. You simply must see a color picture of Mom's gold shiney hineys to fully appreciate it and the other 88 photos in this book.

Color photos are on the website
www.HeatherSharp.com.
Or scan this QR code

In the audiobook, you will hear the actual voices of Bob Tallman, Pat Parelli, Jack Roddy, Jack Sparrowk, Jimmy Roddy, Steve Cosca, Gene St. John Jr., Carla Harrison, Ted Ryan, Brian Sharp, Grant Schlichting, Ryan Schlichting, and Mom and Dad. In this book, those recordings are transcribed.

PRAISE FOR NEVER DULL!

"Inspirational. Be prepared to laugh out loud."
Bob Tallman - 13 time PRCA Announcer of the Year

"Great memories of outstanding people. Well done!"
Jack Roddy - two time World Champion Cowboy

"A fantastic book that shows us attitude is everything. Irish eyes are always smiling. Because of her positive attitude, Marian Sharp thought absolutely anything was possible. I am proud to call her my friend."
Jack Sparrowk -Past President of CattleFax and board member at the National Cowboy and Western Heritage Museum

"Nolan Sharp was what I call a *one-percenter.* I was inspired by him and all the other legends in this book. If you want to fly with eagles, don't hang around turkeys. Associate with the best and forget the rest."
Pat Parelli - Parelli Natural Horsemanship

"A magnificent tribute to the people I loved and who inspired me. Marian was one of those friends that was always in your corner. When I started Road to the Horse, which most people considered an impossible endeavor, Marian encouraged me."
Tootie Bland - Founder of Road to the Horse

"Like smooth Irish Whiskey with a shot of Fireball!" - *Janet Jones*

"A great read. Now more than ever, we need books with people of character. True stories that are told with humor. Be inspired to live a better life." - *Katie Cooney, Author of Wrestling the World*

"Inspirational stories of the people I knew well! Entertaining, and touching. Outstanding!"
  Donnalyn Quintana - President of Western Wishes Foundation

"Bravo!! Very well written. I knew them well and it's hard to believe but it's all true. I laughed until I cried. Very inspirational." - *Leslie Forman*

"Growing up in the Roddy family with all the fun, jokes and shenanigans along with high expectations could not have made a better foundation for life." - Tracy Templeton

"I can verify the crazy antics because I was there. Heather captured it perfectly. You just can't make this up." - *Doug Wheeler*

"Oh my gosh, hilarious! What a great story. It brings back so many memories." - *Katherine Comesana*

"I laughed out loud! I am not a horse person and know nothing about rodeos, but I loved every page. I learned so much, wildly entertaining." -*Karen Ruth*

"I laughed out loud. A good read: aptly titled, funny, and captivating. Lives well lived, with humor, patience, kindness, perseverance and unwavering faith that all things will turn out well." - *Rita Bakken*

ENDORSEMENT

I am so thrilled to endorse this book. My wife Kristen of 54 years, read it and went from laughing out loud to crying. She was enthralled by the great stories that illustrate the values we hold dear.

It's a book that celebrates the people that helped mold my life and have impacted it in so many ways. Heather's uncle, Jack Roddy, Jack Sparrowk, the cowboy hero, Bob Cook who took me in when nobody else would hire me. Marian Sharp and my Pad-na, Nolan Sharp, that's what he called me. We were Team Roping partners. There are many other people that helped me become successful, but these people were the reason for my start.

As they say, it's not about the destination. It's about the journey and who helped you travel on this road.

I was just a kid from Winnemucca, Nevada didn't have a pot to piss in, and wasn't even worried about what window I was gonna throw it out. This was a God wink before it was even a term that we use today. We came from humble beginnings and are now successful. My voice, it is a gift from God. I don't forget where my riches came from. We were blessed by knowing the people that you'll read about in this book or hear as you listen to the audiobook.

We know attitude is everything. *Happy Trails* could have also been the title of this book, but the title *Never Dull* captures the essence of these stories perfectly. It's been a wild ride. I am so, so happy I've been able to be a part of it.

Bob Tallman

The Voice of Professional Rodeo
PRCA Rodeo Announcer of the Year 13 times
Inducted into 15 Halls of Fame

Dedicated to my parents
Life with them was never dull!

Long ago, my dad told me that whom you marry is *the* most important decision you will ever make. It affects your happiness, health, wealth, parents, siblings, kids, job, and every facet of your life.

He told me I should spend some time figuring out what I value and what was important. I wanted someone just like my dad; responsible, easy-going, level-headed, and a straight shooter.

As a young man, Dad wanted someone who didn't smoke or drink and went to church every Sunday, but God had something else in mind for him.

Life with my mom was never dull. The stories in this book will give you a glimpse of what a wild ride it was for 53 years.

Before Mom passed, she and I looked at 83 years of photos and told stories. We laughed hysterically,

I told Mom I was going to write a book, and she said, "Knock yourself out. No one will ever believe it."

"Nice try Mom! I am going to call your friends and they will confirm these stories. Otherwise, people will think I am lying."

"Traitors! Hand me that phone." She thrust out her arthritic hand, "I am going tell them to lie to you."

"HA! Nice try!" I held up the photos victoriously. "I have all these pictures! I'm going to put them in the book too as further evidence that you were a nut!"

She laughed and said, "Oh well, I'll be dead by that time. Do whatever you want.

I said, "Seriously Mom, you had a remarkable life. I am going to write a book. I want people to laugh when they hear these crazy stories, but I also want to share the valuable life lessons that you and Dad taught us."

I learned: you can do anything, be honest, laugh at yourself, fight for what you believe, attitude is everything, stand by your man, you are never too old, there is no such thing as easy money, enjoy the moment and put God first.

MARIAN, NOLAN AND HEATHER - 2007

TABLE OF CONTENTS

My Grandpa John Roddy was born in 1905 in Ireland, He immigrated in 1923 and died in 1984 at 79 years old. In 1935,. he married Ann Burns and almost made it to their 50 year wedding anniversary. They had four children.

- Jack Roddy was born in October 1937 and lives in Texas.
- Nancy Roddy was born in October 1938, and died in October 2013 at 75 years old.
- Marian Roddy was born in May 1940 and died in January 2023. She was almost 83 years old.
- Jimmy Roddy was born in May 1951 and lives in Wyoming.

My dad, Nolan Sharp was born in January 1935. At 29 years old, he married 24-year-old Marian Roddy in 1964.

I was born a few days after Christmas in 1966. Two years later, they were blessed with my brother, Brian.

Dad died in November 2018 at almost 84 years old.

He got to rest in peace for over four years. Mom joined him for eternity on January 13, 2023.

All I've got to say is, "Buckle up, Dude!"

Heaven got another angel, and this one has spurs on.

Chapter 1

LIVE IN THE MOMENT

All good cowboys have a pocket knife clipped on the inside of their front pocket in case a horse gets caught up in a rope. A good horse is hard to come by, and accidents can happen anytime. Always be prepared, no matter what life throws at you.

Marian Roddy went to the 1959 Cow Palace Rodeo to compete in barrel racing. After the rodeo, all the cowboys went to the bar. It was a rowdy place filled with cowboys who were either celebrating or drowning their sorrows after they competed. You had to be very sure of yourself to go in there.

Right after her run, she wanted to celebrate. She put her horse, Chongo, away in his stall, took off her cowboy hat, brushed her long ponytail, and put on some lipstick to go down the street to the Log Cabin Bar. Marian was only 19 but looked almost exactly like her sister Nancy who was 21. Armed with her sister's ID, she elbowed past the cowboys to order a drink at the bar. As she passed steer wrestler John W. Jones, he grabbed her ponytail to pull her back from the bar. "Hey!" She instinctively put her hands on her head.

NEVER DULL!

JOHN W JONES 1963

In one swift motion, John W took out his pocket knife, flicked it open, and cut off her ponytail above the bow. As she spun around, he handed it to her. He said, "Every cowboy in here wants a piece of your tail."

Every woman in the place was mortified, including John W's wife, JoAnn. All the cowboys were howling with laughter. Marian was stunned. She stood there for a second with her mouth hanging open and holding her ponytail. She reached up and ran her fingers through what was left of her hair. She laughed, "Am I on Candid Camera?" She headed for the bathroom. "I've got to look in the mirror. This is a joke, right?" Another barrel racer followed her in and came out to the bar after a few minutes.

A cowboy asked, "Is she crying?"

"No. She sent me out here to get a knife."

Another cowboy asked, "Is she planning a murder or suicide?" The crowd roared. The bartender handed her a pair of scissors. She went back to the bathroom and helped Marian cut her hair.

Marian came out with a new hairdo that looked even cuter than before. She shouted, "Jones is buying the whole bar a round of drinks!" Everyone cheered. Above the roar, she told John W, "And I am drinking for free for the rest of my life!"

Over the years, that story was told many times, and Mom would laugh all over again. "Well, what was I going to do? It was too late. My hair was already gone. Party on!"

What a great attitude. She was always looking forward and never cried over spilled milk. Her mantra was, "Live in the moment; you can't change the past."

That attitude would serve her well for the rest of her life.

Chapter 2

It Was Meant To Be

In the 1960s, record crowds were attending rodeos. Over ten days, 130,000 people paid to watch the events at Cow Palace.

Rodeo was now a spectator sport. Bull riding was and still is a crowd favorite. However, in very close second place was the barrel race. The crowd loved it. Unfortunately, the cowboys were not so impressed. Cowboys called the cowgirls *can chasers* and felt barrel racing was all for show and had nothing to do with skill. The cowboys thought the barrel horses were crazed. "Unsafe at any speed" was the common refrain.

To please the crowd, the rodeo producers enforced a strict dress code. The cowgirls wore brightly colored 'candy straw' cowboys hats, statin shirts with rhinestones, and skin tight lamé pants. To get an idea of their outfits, picture a Las Vegas showgirl costume but with long sleeves. The lamé fabric was very itchy and the women slept with their hair in curlers all night long. Looking good was worth any sacrifice.

At a rodeo in Yuma, Arizona, Jack Sparrowk was the first to call the outfits 'shiny-hineys.' His name will come up again in a few chapters.

Never Dull!

This picture is black and white and you have to imagine the fabulous gold outfit that Mom had on and the robin's egg blue outfit she was holding in her hand. Edie Capps was her good friend for over 60 years. Edie has on handmade lycra pants. The seamstress was unfamiliar with the new material and cut the fabric the wrong way. The pants kept shrinking up.

EDIE CAPPS AND MARIAN RODDY - 1962

IT WAS MEANT TO BE

The following picture shows JoAnn Jones, wife of World Champion Steer Wrestler John W. Jones, wearing a stunning outfit at the National Finals Rodeo Grand Entry in 1963.

Look at that hat!

JOANN JONES - 1963

NEVER DULL!

In 2005, my brother Brian had the foresight to capture their stories on tape. Our parents, Nolan and Marian Sharp, and our uncles, Jack and Jimmy Roddy, were sitting around the table remembering old times.

The following information will help you better understand the transcription.

- The woman they mention is Pat Flanigan. She later becomes a bridesmaid at their wedding.
- *Mount money* means that if someone rides your horse in the rodeo and wins prize money, you get 25% of the winnings.
- Steer wrestling and bull-doggin' are different names for the same thing. The horses are tough as nails and do not have tender mouths because when the steer wrestler backs the horse into the box, the cowboy keeps pressure on the bit. When the cowboy nods and relaxes the pressure on the reins, the horse is ready to go instantly. Like a dragster, the driver has his foot on the gas and releases the clutch, so they have full power from the get-go.
- Mom's good horse is named Chongo, He died of colic two nights before the rodeo in Monterey. The barn got painted with redwood stain, and he chewed on the wood and no one knew the paint was toxic.

BARN PAINTED IN REDWOOD STAIN

MARIAN RODDY RIDING CHONGO AT
CHOWCHILLA BEFORE HE DIED - 1962

NEVER DULL!

Marian

Back in 1954, they were starting to let girls ride in rodeos. They did not have girls' events, so they started the girls' barrel racing. And I was 18 years old. I went to the Redwood City Rodeo for my very first barrel race, and I won fourth, and that was a big deal. And then, I got a little better and joined the Girls Rodeo Association. You had to win $200 to join at that time. So I won my $200. I got my first Girls Rodeo Association card, and I think I was Number 232. I don't know how many thousands there have been since then. And then I made it every year to the California Barrel Racing Finals. I did not win first place, but I was usually in there. And then, in 1961, I made it to the National Finals. It was in Santa Maria, and I was in 14th place.

Marian

So how I met Nolan is . . .

Jack

I'm the one who did that.

Marian

Yeah, he's taking credit for all of this.

Jack

Well, I did. If it wasn't for me, you'd gotten nowhere!

Marian

IT WAS MEANT TO BE

HA! I was entered at the rodeo in Monterey, and then two nights before that, Chongo got colic, and he died. I am now without a horse, and I'm devastated. And I was entered at the Monterey Rodeo, and Jack said, "Oh gosh, poor Marian." And I said, "I've already entered, and I'm going to have to pay my entry fees." He said, "Well, you could take Brownie."

Jack

I did.

Marian

Well, that's a fine idea, but Brownie's a bull-doggin' horse.

Jack

And Brownie came off the racetrack. He'd never been bulldogged on before. Two weeks later, I won Sonora and Salinas on him right off the racetrack.

Marian

So I get him in the arena that night up at the ranch, and I'm pulling him around the barrels, and I think, okay, well, I'm entered and paid my entry fees. Pat's planning to pick me up. We go down, and I'm the third girl out. So I am dragging him around these barrels, and guess what? They missed my time. And he wasn't really bad. I think I had a pretty good time. So I think, oh, my God. Now I got to do that again. Well, now he knows where the outgate is, and he has no mouth.

Jimmy

NEVER DULL!

I was there to watch the wreck. I was 11.

Marian

That's right, you were there, Jim. So I have to run him again. So I'm running him around, jerking him around these barrels, and there's this girl on a big black stud sitting at the outgate. And I holler at her, "I can't stop this horse! Get out of the way!" She doesn't pay any attention to me. I go straight into her, and I go over the top. Her horse goes down, and Brownie goes down. When he tries to get up, his shoulder is dislocated. And I heard Jimmy Rodriquez say, "Oh my God, her brother's going to kill her!" because they knew it was Brownie. So the vet comes over and says, "It's a dislocated shoulder. This horse will never be any good. We need to put him down."

I said, "No." I put him in the trailer and cried all the way to Valley Vet Hospital with Pat Flanigan. My dad always said, "Use the older vet, Dr. Hilton. Don't use any of those young dummies."

And so out comes the young dummy on a Sunday. I said, "Is Dr. Hilton here?" The hired man said, "No, he doesn't work on Sundays." I said, "Well, we have to have Dr. Hilton. Because my dad said . . ." I sounded like this little rich Roddy girl. I said, "Oh, I have to have Dr. Hilton because I've got a horse down with a broken shoulder."

He said, "We have a young veterinarian here."

I said, "Oh, he can only look at my horse, but he can't touch him." So we unload Brownie, and outcomes Nolan, and wouldn't you know, on Brownie's trip home, he popped his shoulder back in.

Brownie was a short horse, only fourteen-one. And Nolan says, "Well, I'm just going to hop on this horse so that I can look down on his shoulders." He got on bareback, and he's looking down on the shoulders, and he's walking him around. I'm thinking, God, maybe he's a cowboy. He got on that horse real easy. He says, "You know, I really don't see anything wrong with this horse." I had mascara running down my face and shiny pants, which we used to call the shiny-hineys.

Nolan

So then she noticed I didn't have a ring on.

Marian

He had no ring on, and it was Sunday afternoon, so we put the horse in the trailer. And I mentioned to Pat, "Oh, he was a good-looking young guy, and he didn't have a ring. He should be home with his family on Sunday."

So anyway, we go up to the ranch. Jack and everybody's waiting for me to come home from Monterey because he's going to Sacramento State Fair the next day. I put the horse in a stall, and then I went back to the house, and they said, So how did you do? I said, I won third.

"Really?"

Never Dull!

"But there was a little problem," because I knew he was going to hear it from the ropers. I said, "I had a little run-in with this girl when I was going out the gate." Jack goes, "You did what?"

I said, "He's fine, he's fine." So we all go walking over to the barn, and I go in and put his halter on and take him out. Well, there was a little step coming out of our barn. What does Brownie do? He falls to his knees in front of everybody. Down he goes! Now he's got his knees all scraped up.

Jack

No mount money, horse fallin' down. (laughter)

Marian

So I load him up the next day. You hooked up my car and trailer, Jack, and you said to get him to Sacramento because everybody will use him for bull-doggin'. You hooked up my trailer, and you plugged in. I asked you, "Is everything okay? Because I don't know much about this."

You said, "Yes, it's all okay." I get outside of Milpitas, and I look at the rear tires, and they are burning. And I pull over, pop Brownie out of there, and my tires are now on fire. Edie and I are throwing dirt on them. Some guy comes along, feels sorry for us, we get his trailer, and he brings me up to Sacramento. By now, the rodeo is over, and I go pulling in as Bob Maynard, Hollywood Bob, sees me coming in. He says, "Your brother's going to kill you. The bulldogging had just ended."

Jack

How come I didn't kill you?

Marian

I don't know. (laughter)

Jack

Because I got no mount money, didn't win money in Sacramento because I didn't have a horse. It's all your fault. (laughter)

Marian

Oh, you were off to another rodeo by that time. (laughter)

JOHN RODDY HAZING FOR JACK RODDY

Chapter 3

THE GUY IN THE GLASS

Until my dad, Nolan Sharp, met Mom, he had no experience with horses besides reading about them in vet school. When he was a boy, they had a cow for milk and he raised pigs to put himself through college, but the closest he came to a horse was a mule in Korea.

He was born in 1935 in Eaton, Colorado, and graduated from high school in 1953 in Shelbyville, Tennessee. He went to the University of Tennessee at Knoxville for undergrad and then Auburn Veterinary School.

He joined the Army right after graduation from vet school and was stationed in Korea near the Demilitarized Zone and the 38th parallel. He took care of 450 German Shepherds trained as attack dogs to patrol the DMZ.

I guess in the DMZ, you couldn't have a gun or a weapon, but you could have a dog.

Some of you are old enough to remember the TV show M*A*S*H, which was based on real life. In one episode, Colonel Potter had a horse. In reality, the general had a mule.

NEVER DULL!

Dad got woke up late one night because the general's mule had colic. The general worried his beloved steed would twist a gut and die.

Horses or mules can't belch or vomit. The typical treatment was to pass a tube down the mule's throat and into his stomach. The tube would provide a way for the gas to escape and relieve pressure. Then the vet would pour mineral oil down the tube to lube things up. Soon the mule would feel better and be able to poop again.

To get the supplies he needed, Dad had to wake up the cranky supply sergeant in the wee hours of the morning. Dad was stressed, and the sergeant was in a bad mood. Dad was focused on the animal, and his people skills were not the best.

The sergeant put on his fatigues and muttered, "This had better not be a joke. Who's ever heard of a vet needing something from me in the middle of the night."

Dad said, "I need eight feet of one-inch plastic tubing and a gallon of mineral oil."

The sergeant growled, "What the hell do you need that for?"

Dad could have pulled rank and told him to follow orders. Instead, he said, "I'm going to shove it up the general's ass."

The sergeant was speechless.

Dad grinned, "Hurry up. He's full of shit."

I learned from that story that it's sometimes faster to use humor than toss your weight around and pull rank.

The following is transcribed from my sons, Grant and Ryan, speaking at their grandfather Nolan's Celebration of Life.

THE GUY IN THE GLASS

Ryan

I'm going to start off with something that Nolan's sister Sylvia once shared with me, but she couldn't be here today. The one thing that always stuck in her head about Nolan was how much everyone liked him when they were growing up. In a span of one and a half years, they went to three different high schools. And in all three high schools, Nolan was part of the popular kids.

At their final high school, he was elected to NHS, the National Honor Society. He was the vice president of the senior class, and he was elected the Duke of Personality. But there's more. He was the president of the FFA (Future Farmers of America) as well. All within a year of getting there. That's pretty dang impressive.

And she always said that her claim to fame in high school was that she was Nolan's little sister. I mean, I kind of have that with Grant here, so I feel her pain. (Laughter) Brother! I am the little brother! I'm not the little sister, just to clarify.

And she said that in their senior year, they both joined the Methodist Church Youth Center. Spelled METH Youth Center in her letter to me. And she said that she had a lot of fun with him in high school, and she'll never forget those days.

Grant

I remember for my eighth birthday, we were out riding somewhere in Colorado, and all I wanted to

NEVER DULL!

1997

do was camp with Nolan. I wanted to be in his tent, just him and me, because every year, there's a poem he would like to read, The Cremation of Sam McGee. This poem he just loved. So every year, I'd read it. "Sam McGee is from Tennessee. Where the cotton blooms and blows wide, left his home down south to go up north, nobody knows." And Grandpa would smile, and it made me so happy. And the reason why we all flocked as grandkids to Grandpa was because of just the man he was.

I mean, most of our time in childhood was spent with Grandma because she was loud and a Roddy, and who would have thought... from Grandma? (laughter) But we all knew (laughter)... Grandpa was the smartest. (laughter)

So there's a story that all of Grandpa's siblings like to tell. When he was in high school, he said, "I'm never going to marry a woman that smokes or dyes her hair." And he got both!

We had a Sharp reunion a couple of years ago, and we were in the car with Nolan's sister, Sylvia. When I was young, I heard all these stories about the Roddys, larger-than-life cowboys. So I turned to her and asked, do the Sharps have any stories of prohibition or bootlegging? (laughter)

There was a big difference between Grandpa and Grandma, as we talked about, with their upbringing, but that difference... is what held them together.

He loved Grandma all the way through to the end of 54 years. And the reason for that is three things about Grandpa stick out.

He was a man of integrity, of service, and of excellence. He was a man of character. So no matter where he was as a veterinarian, he always did the right thing. He was always serving others, whether it was when he was in Korea or with his community.

NEVER DULL!

He never grew up in this cowboy lifestyle. He was not of the cowboy world but in it. And it's like how the Lord calls us to come down to this earth, not to be of this world but in the world. He was a man of character that isn't seen a lot in a lot of cowboy communities.

There's a poem that I always read to myself, and I memorized when I went off to basic, The Guy in the Glass, and you can see it on the back side of your pamphlet. And I had this memorized when I was out there, and it just really speaks a lot to Grandpa's character,

Because you can fool the whole world down the pathway of years and get pats on the back as you pass, but your final reward will be heartaches and tears if you cheated the guy in the glass.

And I think Grandpa lived this poem every day of his life because I think when he ended up, he looked at the glass and knew he did something great with his life.

THE GUY IN THE GLASS

The Guy in the Glass by Dale Wimbrow

When you get what you want in your struggle for self,
And the world makes you King for a day,
Then go to the mirror and look at yourself,
And see what that guy has to say.
For it isn't your Father, or Mother, or Wife,
Who judgment upon you must pass.
The feller whose verdict counts most in your life
Is the guy staring back from the glass.
He's the feller to please, never mind all the rest,
For he's with you clear up to the end,
And you've passed your most dangerous, difficult test
If the guy in the glass is your friend.
You may be like Jack Horner and "chisel" a plum,
And think you're a wonderful guy,
But the man in the glass says you're only a bum
If you can't look him straight in the eye.
You can fool the whole world down the pathway of years,
And get pats on the back as you pass,
But your final reward will be heartaches and tears
If you've cheated the guy in the glass.

NEVER DULL!

We all need to think about the guy in the glass. Something else I learned from my parents was: We have no idea how we might impact someone's life. We are responsible to God to be kind and encourage others.

After my parents died, many people contacted me to tell me how Mom and Dad had affected their lives. One woman said, "Your mom told me I could do anything. She told me to follow my dreams. My life was changed because of her." Another said, "Your parents were a big deal. I was a nobody. They had nothing to gain by being nice to me, and I will never forget that."

We also need to be aware that young people are watching us. As an adult, you have incredible power to influence young minds.

When Mom was nine years old, a chance encounter sparked a dream. A friend of Mom's parents was a flight attendant for TWA and came to visit the ranch in San Jose. She just flew in from Honolulu and still had her uniform on. She brought everyone fresh flower leis and chocolate-covered macadamia nuts when she arrived. Mom was awe-struck when the tall, beautiful blond put the lei around Mom's neck and kissed each cheek. The kindness of that woman changed Mom's life.

At that time, it was believed that women only went to college to get their MRS degree. The common wisdom was that if girls weren't lucky enough to be homemakers, they could be a hairdresser, a nurse, work in a bank, or become a secretary.

If a girl was really lucky, she could become an airline stewardess. But if you were married, you had to quit. You would decide what is most important to you, your family, or your career?

It would take Mom another 40 years before she realized her dream and became the oldest flight attendant American Airlines had ever hired at that point.

God didn't answer her prayer to become a flight attendant as fast as she would have liked, but he did send her a fantastic husband. After Mom and Dad met on that fateful day when the horse dislocated his shoulder, Dad often came to the ranch to doctor cattle.

Marian

We had a cow with foot rot, and Nolan's out there treating the cow. And says to Jack, I just got out of the Army, and I haven't been married, and I'm looking for someone to date. And Jack said, "Oh, you should try my sister if you don't like her. She's got some friends."

Jack

I got a bunch of sisters. Take your pick! (laughter)

Marian

So then he called me maybe a week or two later and asked me to go to a basketball game. And I went to an all-girls school. I didn't know anything about basketball. Horses, I knew a little. So I said, "Oh, I LOVE basketball." So he picks me up in a brand-new car. You had a brand-new Pontiac. And Jimmy, my brother, goes running out. He came back and said, "Oh, he's got a great new car, and this guy's really cool." We go to the basketball game in San Francisco, and guess what? Out of the whole crowd, we won the basketball signed by Wilt Chamberlain. That was the first time he had ever won anything, so he thought that was good luck.

Nolan

So then we go to a Cattleman's Dinner, and I won a bottle of whiskey.

Marian

So again, he thought, this is pretty good luck.

Jack

Ugh, if he only knew. (laughter)

Nolan

So then I proposed. First, there was a cow that had milk fever. So I had a little short rope. So luckily, I roped her and tied her head to her leg, and I gave her a shot of penicillin.

Marian

My dad was so impressed. He said, "Well if he catches her, what the hell is he going to do with her?" But she was so weak that he was able to pull her down and tie her up.

Nolan

Yeah. So then I proposed to Marian. And the next day, I went up to the ranch looking everywhere for that cow, and I said, "I think that cow is dead."

Marian

You were looking down in the gully.

Nolan

I'm walking around. All of a sudden, the fog clears, and here's the sun shining on this cow. So then I go down to the bar to get John's permission. Jack is tending the bar, and John's playing Pedro with Zim, the bookkeeper. And so Jack calls Marian, and he whispers, "Hey, I think there's something going on. I think he's going to propose to you."

Marian

I already know! (laughter)

Nolan

I said, John, the cow's okay. I want to have Marian's hand. And John says, "Oh good, I thought I'd never get rid of her. Have at her."

Mom and Dad were a great combo. As someone recently said, "You can't think of one without thinking of the other. They were quite a pair." Dad was serious, and Mom lightened him up and made him laugh. He was sensible and practical, and she was spontaneous and fun. He was her anchor, and she spiced up his life. He would have been content leading a conventional life, doctoring cows, and having homemade meals every night. He didn't have big aspirations.

Mom wanted excitement but also knew the value of a good man. They got married on August 30, 1964.

NEVER DULL!

JIMMY, JACK, MARIAN, ANN, JOHN, NANCY,
TRACY AND DAN TEMPLETON

THE GUY IN THE GLASS

Many years after John W Jones cut off Mom's ponytail and handed it to her, all four Roddy siblings were at a party with John W. He told Mom, "The deal is off. Now I'm drinking for free. You owe me."

Mom stomped her foot, feigning outrage at the injustice of all of this. She was not sure what he was talking about, so she pretended that she was so mad she was speechless.

John W told her, "I did you a favor. That ponytail was dragging you down, Horseface. Nolan would have never had a second look. I'm the reason you got married."

Now the hollering began. Her brother Jack Roddy shouted, "That's not true! I fixed them up. It was all me."

Her sister, Nancy Roddy, pushed them out of the way. "That is wrong! I told Marian that if she didn't marry him, she would be an idiot. I'm the one that did it."

Her young brother, Jimmy Roddy, then protested, "Nope! I was there on the very first day they met."

I don't want to sell you a bill of goods and say everything was perfect with the relationship with her family. It wasn't always rainbows and unicorns with Mom. Jack, Nancy, Jimmy, and even me, each got a turn in the barrel when she wasn't speaking to us. Not for a few hours or a few days. Sometimes it lasted for a few years. In the end, though, she did make peace with everyone.

What I learned from that is, *No storm lasts forever.*

NEVER DULL!

JACK, NANCY, MARIAN AND JIMMY - 2007

Chapter 4

$18 TO MILLIONAIRE

My grandpa, John Roddy, was born in Ireland and immigrated to America when he was 18 and had $18 in his pocket. Before he was 45, he would become a millionaire.

My uncle Jack would become a World Champion Cowboy in 1966 and 1968.

We all know how important grit, tenacity, and perseverance are. But I think the most important thing is attitude. My uncle calls it heart. He said that people who win have heart, no matter where they come from or what they do—golf, Olympics, ping-pong, whatever. If they have heart, they are going to win.

The definition of heart is hard to explain. If they have heart, they have desire or drive. Heart means they will keep going when other people quit. All they think about is getting better. I guess it is similar to a hunger. It is a burning in your belly that can't be put out. Your circumstances do not define who you are.

NEVER DULL!

You can't describe it or put your finger on it, but you have seen it. Firefighters have it. People in the military have it. Even some everyday people have it. The checker at the grocery store, your son's second-grade teacher, the stay-at-home mom you work out with—they all have heart.

Having heart doesn't mean you are selfish, mean, or callous. I have seen plenty of nice people with heart. It means you won't quit. Nothing is going to stop you. The term heart is often used to describe a racehorse. A horse that will dig down deep and find that extra something that pushes his nose across the finish line first.

My grandpa, John Roddy had heart. He was born in 1905 in a one-room thatched cottage with dirt floors on the family farm in Country Roscommon, Ireland. He was the second of seven children. Because there were no prospects of work in Ireland, John's father, Michael, went to America to make money to send home. Tragically, he died at 47 years old.

John had an older brother, who also died. Now John was the most senior of the family. He quit school in the fourth grade and became the man of the house. Thirteen is much too young to be all grown up, but he rose to the challenge. Late at night, John read stories about Cowboys and Indians, cattle and buffalo. and dreamed of becoming a cowboy.

The following is a transcript of Jack Roddy talking about his dad.

> This is a story about a legend, my father, John Roddy. And I gotta say something, all of us in life have been successful, and it came from my father.

Because he said one thing, there's no such thing as CAN'T. And all of us believe in that. I especially believed in that. His father immigrated from Ireland when my dad was still in grade school. To describe my father's home, it was a dirt floor, rock walls three feet thick, and a thatched roof. The fire in that house had never been out for 900 years. They carried water for 200 feet. There was no running water, and the pigs farrowed in the house. So that was poverty in Ireland, as my father knew it. He was the first in the family to go to school.

My dad's father, Michael Roddy, died when Dad was in the fourth grade. The family farm in Ireland was 40 acres. They raised a couple of cows and a handful of chickens. Everything was done on the barter system. They had dairy cows. They would milk. When the cow had a calf, they took it to town to sell on Tuesday in Ballaghaderreen, and that's where they got their money for clothes. They lived off the land. When he was 14, he quit school. He had a fourth-grade education and went to work, and he took care of the family.

Several years ago, I went to the Hall of Fame in Oklahoma City, and I was asked about my love of the West. And I said I can attribute my love of the West to my father because when he was a little boy in Ireland, he used to read books about the West, cowboys, and Indians. He couldn't wait 'til someday he could go to America.

NEVER DULL!

My grandpa John's cousins, Patrick and Micheal Roddy, left Ireland for greener pastures and more opportunities. Patrick wrote home about the large ranch he owned in California. As is often the case, the Irish tell tall tales. In John's mind, the ranch was hundreds of acres with thousands of cattle.

JOHN RODDY - 1923

FROM $18 TO A MILLIONAIRE

At 18, John boarded a ship to Ellis Island with no belongings other than his life savings of 18 dollars in his pocket. He worked in Philadelphia as a landscaper for a year to save up money. And he then made his way across the country to find his cousins. The ranch was really a 20-acre potato patch with four sheep, six ducks, and a couple of chickens near San Francisco.

Those potatoes would change John's life. John was resourceful, a creative thinker, and he never gave up. The potatoes would later be used to make alcohol during prohibition. And Grandpa became a bootlegger.

I asked my Uncle Jimmy, "Other than the fact that he was a hard worker, how did Grandpa become a millionaire at 46? That was a lot of money back then. Now everyone who owns a 1/4 acre in the Bay Area is a millionaire, but one million then is worth eleven million today. How did that happen?"

Jimmy Roddy tells the story about his dad, John:

Well, it was because of Big Mike Roddy. He was the first guy that came over from the old country and he was an ice hauler. He made good money hauling ice. See, Dad was partners with Mike on a whiskey still at Pedro Point. It was up on a hill. Because of the smell of the sour mash, you couldn't make whiskey in town. You can make gin in town, but not whiskey.

You can smell it still from a long way off if it's whiskey. It was out of town, right by the ocean. The still belonged to his cousin Big Mike Roddy. So

35

they're out there making stuff and on the side of this hill, there were strawberries all the way up to the top. So here come the trucks coming up. And his cousin Mike Roddy said, By God, it's a Federal Men. We better run. Let's get out of here."

And Dad says, "I think it's the strawberry growers."

And Mike says, "Oh, you know it all, don't you? You big Mick, you know it all. Well, you stay right here. Right here, you bloody Eegit! We're leaving. You deal with the Federal men. "

And my dad stayed there. They were the strawberry trucks and my dad had the biggest whiskey still in San Francisco.

You can imagine that caused a big argument between the two cousins. John kept the still because he said that he hung in there when Big Mike fled. And John pointed out that if Mike was a man of his word he would stick by what he said.

Without your word and your integrity, you are nothing.

So now John was bootlegging whiskey but that wasn't enough. He wanted to expand and he bought some more stills.

Jimmy tells the rest of the story:

Where he made the vodka and gin, he had flats and he'd rent you one of the flats and for real cheap. Well, he was downstairs making the gin at one place and the vodka at the other place. He had four different places. Then he said, "OK, Heather, when the water man comes, you call me."

And so the water man says to you, "How come you use so much water?"

You say, "Well, I have two kids and my husband, and we use a lot of water."

"Well, you're using a lot of water. You're using way too much water."

So you'd call, the old man would go and take the thing apart and take it over to my house, and two days later, guess who showed up? The cops? So then they take it to my place.

Then the water man would knock on my door. He would say, "How come you're using so much water?"

"Well, I've got three kids, and a wife takes four showers a day."

"Well, I don't believe you."

So he takes the still apart and takes it back to your place.

The deal was the cops will show up 2 to 3 days after the water man came,

If you are making booze it was a great time to be Irish with all the Irish cops. He was also paying the cops off with hooch and some cash on the side to encourage them to keep their mouths shut.

The parents of John's future wife, Ann Burns also immigrated from Ireland. Ann was born on the boat and would automatically become a citizen wherever the ship first docked. Thank goodness the ship made it to America, the land of the free and the home of the brave. Otherwise, things would have been a lot different. I am told that the voyage was harrowing.

Ann's dad was a successful carpenter in San Francisco. He made a lot of money and started buying property overlooking the ocean. All his friends thought it was too far away, and he was nuts. Unfortunately, he lost it all during the Great Depression. In 1929, Ann tried to get a job as a secretary and saw the sign INNA - which meant *Irish or Italians need not apply*. She was also a quick thinker and changed the spelling of her name to Byrnes and got the job.

John was 30 years old before he met Ann Burns at an Irish dance in South San Francisco. 30 was ancient at that time. He was probably too busy running booze and did not have a chance to date.

John married Ann shortly after they met and had four children, Jack in 1937, Nancy in 1938, Marian in 1940, and 11 years later, when Ann was 44 and John was 46, they had Jimmy in 1951.

John started with nothing and became a millionaire. He owned four bars in San Francisco, including the longest bar in the world, bought several ranches in San Jose, and fulfilled his dream of becoming a cowboy.

Jack Roddy continues:

When prohibition was repealed, he bought a 12-stool beer and wine joint on Third and Howard, which was the toughest part of San Francisco. In those days, it was called the Barbary Coast. It was a seaport, and ships from all over the United States came to San Francisco. It was the habit of bar owners to rob sailors or teamsters. The sailors would get drunk, and they would rob them.

But my dad had a good reputation. He promised safety. If a sailor came in off his ship and got drunk, the bartender was trained to take their money away from them, put a note in their pocket, and lock their money up in the safe.

The man would wake up in the morning and see the note, "Your money is at Roddy's." The sailor would come in, and they were handed their money. Daddy had a reputation for honesty.

In those days in San Francisco, right after the depression, people were poor, and a lot of big, tough men tried to be prize fighters to feed their families, and they'd walk into a bar and take it over.

They didn't walk into a bar with my dad. The guy that worked with my dad for 40 years was Sammy Freed. He said, "If a fight started, your father would jump over the bar with one hand and knock 'em out. He was his own law and order, so people felt safe. They felt it was an honest place to do business."

He bought another bar directly across the street, and he bought a liquor store. His business grew. Then he bought a bar at 1099 Mission. His business further grew.

Then in 1937, there was a bar for sale called Bradley's in the Fillmore district, between Geary and Post. It was the longest bar in the world.

My father decided he had to do something different. So they designed a beer glass, like a fish bowl. They served 14oz of beer for a nickel when they opened. It was a tremendous success. The bar was a city block long. There were seven bartenders in one shift. They called it Roddy's Fishbowl, and that's been our family cattle brand. It was registered in 1942.

There were two things to see in those days in San Francisco. One was the Golden Gate Bridge that opened in 1939, and the other was the longest bar in the world, which at that time, had the tallest bartender in the world, who was seven foot four, and the shortest, who was four-foot somethin'.

People came to see the longest bar in the world when they opened the Golden Gate Bridge. Daddy belonged to the San Mateo County Sheriff's Posse, and they rode across the bridge down Market Street and rode 56 horses in that bar at one time.

Going back to Daddy's love of the West. Mom and Dad would ride through Golden Gate Park, and Daddy met our first World Champion, Charlie Maggini, in 1929, and Maggini got him involved with the Western way of life.

JOHN RODDY, SAN
MATEO POSSE 1936

ANN RODDY CARRYING THE FLAG SAN
MATEO POSSE - 1936

NEVER DULL!

SAN MATEO POSSE - 1936

So pretty soon, Daddy bought a rodeo grounds in Colma, California. He also put on the first rodeo at the World's Fair Exposition at Treasure Island in 1939.

When they opened the Golden Gate Bridge, Charlie Maggini had a horse of my dad's called Johnny Biggs. After they rode 56 horses in the bar, there were carpets on the floor. Maggini backed his horse up, over and undered him, ran him down the bar, set him, and dug the rugs up.

When 56 horses rode into the bar, they lined up 27 horses head to tail inside the bar. My Uncle Jimmy took his one horse into 24 different bars but he could not beat Grandpa's record.

FULL PAGE AD IN SAN FRANCISCO NEWSPAPER - 1937

NEVER DULL!

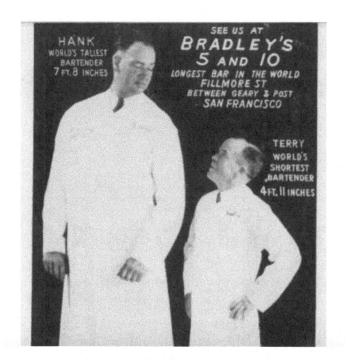

TALLEST AND SHORTEST BARTENDERS

JOHN RODDY BAR OWNER

FROM $18 TO A MILLIONAIRE

Never Dull!

JOHN RODDY - 1941

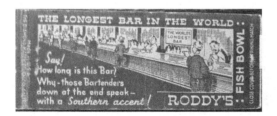

Match Book Cover

FROM $18 TO A MILLIONAIRE

Grandpa John wanted his family in Ireland to come to America and see the ranch.

Jimmy tells the story of when John's brother James and his wife Mary came over.

Dad paid for James and Mary's trip to California and they had never been anywhere. They had never been to Dublin. They had never been anywhere in Ireland except for the main town in their county. Heck, they've hardly been in any cars. So they take a bus to Shannon airport, they get through, and she knew my dad loves duck eggs. So she loaded the duck eggs. They get on the plane, they land in New York. They're going through customs, they opened her bags, and the agent said, "Ma'am, what are these?"

She says, "They're duck eggs. I'm taking them to Big John Roddy. He loves duck eggs."

He says, "Ma'am, we don't know if they're fresh." And you know, you couldn't get anything through. But she was just never been anywhere except for the farm.

She says, "Of course they are. The ducks just laid him this morning."

And the Customs guy knew how innocent she was. The guy could tell, she wasn't a secret agent or a drug runner and he closed the suitcase. And the next morning, my dad was eating duck eggs from Ireland.

NEVER DULL!

My dad, Nolan gave the eulogy at Grandpa John Roddy's funeral. Dad was normally a very quiet guy, the opposite of all the Roddys, who spoke loud and all at once. Dad was elected to speak because the family knew they would be too choked up to speak at the funeral. When I cleaned out their house for the last time, I found the typed script for the eulogy in Dad's desk with notes in the margin in my mother's handwriting.

The first line was typed by my dad. It said, "On behalf of the Roddy family, we are glad you are here." And then in my mother's handwriting in blue pen. "After all these years, I finally have a chance to talk," I remember that got a big laugh from everyone in the Catholic Church.

Dad was quiet but not shy. He was very comfortable behind the microphone and gave a fantastic summary of John's life.

I won't bore you with the first part of the eulogy. It said many of the same things you just read. I will just give you the new stuff.

My dad, Nolan continued:

John's bar business was so successful because he cared about his patrons. His bars were for the working class, the men who kept America moving. His bars grew because the men trusted him and knew their money was safe. While cleaning John's office we came across a piece of paper with a quote from Abraham Lincoln: God must have loved the plain people because he made so many of them."

He dreamed of being a cowboy. After being a successful bar owner, he bought a ranch in San Jose.

He never strayed far from his Western way of life except to take all important trips back to Ireland. Each time he went, he would take one of his four kids back to the family farm. In Ireland, he was treated like one of the heroes in the Nickel Novels. They respected and admired Big John. That's when his kids realized what a great man their father was. He had come from such humble beginnings with only a fourth-grade education to start fresh in an unknown country. Upon returning home, they put their father on a pedestal he deserved.

Through hard work and determination, John fulfilled his dreams.

Dinners at the Roddy Ranch were a special treat. I am still amazed, so many people can talk at one time and understand each other. Politics and religion were usually discussed. John always came away with the last word because he was the loudest and would pound his fist on the table. Many of you here are able to remember a conversation with John three days later because of the ache in your shoulder when he poked you with his finger. Because by God man, he wanted you to understand.

NEVER DULL!

John was passionate about what he believed. He loved America and valued honesty and hard work. We will all miss John."

Everyone in the crowd nodded. Dad folded his script, came from behind the podium and walked somberly to the casket in the center aisle. Dad stood there for a moment with his head bowed in prayer and then gently placed his hand on the casket.

He said, "Rest in Peace, John." It was very touching. There was not a dry eye in the place.

Then Dad pounded on the casket three times like he was punching John's shoulder, "And now John, by God, I have the last word."

The altar boys jumped when Dad pounded and everyone in the church laughed. The alter boys thought Dad was being disrespectful and were unaware of the Irish Tradition of three knocks.

From $18 to a Millionaire

Jimmy Roddy talks about his Dad and his notorious finger punching you in the shoulder:

> Even the cops, or the sheriffs on patrol, used to tell each other to look out or he will knock a hole in your shoulder. And everybody in the bar knew that you better not have a bad shoulder or it will hurt.

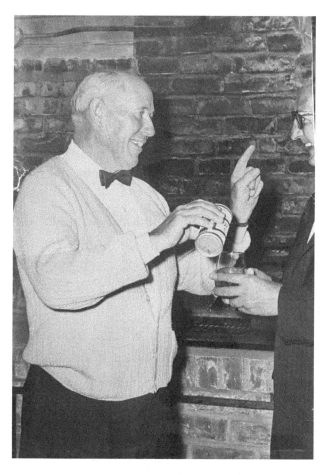

JOHN RODDY 1965

Never Dull!

Jimmy talks about going to Ireland with his Dad:

When Dad and I went to Ireland, I was 11. And we were walking down the main street of Ballaghaderreen. And here came a horse-drawn hearse and we were walking towards it. He grabbed me by the neck and said, "Here's what is going to happen, when the hearse goes by, we turn and take three steps with the coffin to show respect. And I said, "Dad, did you know him?" The old man said, "I don't have to know him. We just have to show respect." So here came the coffin. We took our three steps, we stopped, the hearse went on, we turned back around and went on our way. And then he said, "When you go by the coffin in the church, for really dear friends and family members, tap on the coffin three times. Three taps for love, honor and respect."

What I learned from my Grandpa was never forget where you came from. No matter how much money you have, always value the working man and treat everyone with respect. Grandpa was rewarded for honesty. Once trust is gone, you can never get it back.

Grandpa loved America and what it stood for. He came here looking for an opportunity, not a handout. Nobody owes you anything. He valued the Western way of life and everything it represents. By his example, we learned the value of resilience, grit, hard work, get back up when you get knocked down. And never quit.

Chapter 5

THE RODDY RANCH

After John sold the bars in San Francisco, he opened a bar in San Jose called *The Boots and Saddles*. He bought a 1200-acre ranch in the San Jose foothills on Sierra Road.

RODDY RANCH 1950

NEVER DULL!

The Roddys had been richly blessed. There was a lot of hard work, but there was also a lot of being in the right place and the right time. Was it the luck of the Irish? Hard work? Or Divine intervention? Or all three?

Big John was known for being loud and extroverted, but he quietly gave large sums of money to the Sisters of the Carmelite Mission. He financed a large part of the Monastery in San Jose. He knew that he had received a blessing from God. The money was God's all along. John just got to use it for a while. He was returning what was first given to him.

Jack Roddy tells stories about his dad.

In 1950, Daddy bought four bulls at the Red Bluff Sale. They are halter broke and gentle. He tells me, "I'll be going to San Francisco for a month. I want you to feed these bulls every day, give them less and less and get them ready for breeding season, okay?" He's gone to San Francisco. The first thing I do is run them in the barn. They all had halters on. I tied one to the fence, put my bull rope on, and bucked them. And they just trotted, they were fat. We go across the corral: plop, plop, plop. So I ride four of them every day.

Well, the corrals are gravel, their feet start to hurt, and pretty soon, they start to get mad. And three weeks later, I'd run them in the barn, and they're trying to hook at me then. Tie 'em up. Daddy had a big Tom Mix hat. And I took that hat. I'm about 13 years old and chaps on, and I get on this bull. I got my bull rope on, tighten the flank up, and I pull the rope. That sucker goes across the pen. They've learned to buck a little bit. (laughter)

And all of a sudden, he stopped, and my Tom Mix hat hit the ground. The short-horned bull slung his head and came up with my hat. It was a foggy morning, and I thought, "If this guy kills me, they might never find me."

A long story short, three or four days later, Daddy comes back after a month in San Francisco to see his prize bulls. He opens the gate, and those four alligators took a run at him. They had flank marks, spur marks. My little self got whipped.

But then the real whippin' happened because you were there, Marian!

Johnny Biggs won the Cow Palace. That horse was really broke. And he was kind of a snaky horse but broke. And every time my parents had guests, I'd always put them on that horse, and they seem to fall off. So Daddy told me, he said, "Whatever you do, don't put anybody on Johnny."

So we are down at the house, and there's a big, fat Scotch lady, and she told me about all her riding experience, how she used to ride in Scotland. I said, "Really?'

"Yeah."

"You ride a lot."

"Yep."

"You would like to ride?"

NEVER DULL!

"Oh! I'd love to ride."

"Okay." So I hot foot it up to the barn. And I get that big bridle horse and I bring her this horse. She has her English breeches on. She has glasses, she has a hearing aid. I say, "Here's a horse."

She crawls on him, and the first thing she does is go, "Yah!" And that sucker went down to the bottom, wide open with this lady hanging on the horse's neck. He goes clear down where there was a fig tree! He goes under the fig tree. And I thought, Oh, my God. Oh boy, here come Daddy. The whole pack of us run down. I'll never forget this as long as I live. We run down there. My heart's poundin'. (laughter) This is where it gets funny.

She's down on her hands and knees, and I'm laughing. She gets up and has her glasses hanging down, her hair falling down, and her hearing aids down here. And she stands up, and I'm laughing. She said, "I guess you've seen everything now."

But what she didn't know was her pants fell down around her knees. And my Old Man looked at me. (laughter) That night when everybody left, he walked into the room. Oh man, I got beat pretty severely.

THE RODDY RANCH

Mom was eleven years old when she learned what the words ill repute, prostitution, and retraction meant. What an education. She didn't learn that in Catholic school.

John bought another ranch with an old farmhouse about a mile and a half past Roddy Ranch on Sierra Road. They called it The Anderson Place. John rented it out to what seemed to be a nice lady. She was very friendly and paid the rent in cash. Hmmm, small bills. Imagine that?

Marian

Jack, tell the story about the little house.

Jimmy

Yeah? How come you're always in the bad ones?

Jack

Oh dear, you sure you want to hear this? (Embarrassed.) OK. Daddy bought a place up back on Sierra Road called the Anderson, with a fallin' down house on it.

Marian

Yep.

Jack

So I'm a young man. I was going to high school, and I kept noticing all this traffic up down the road, and I started seeing red signs on trees.

Marian

Yeah, they were cans, painted red.

Jack

And I thought this thing sounds suspicious. I go back one night, and I camp there (laughter). And cars pull in, lights in the yard would go on, and then the drivers would duck in there. AH-HA! It's a whore house. So I get all my buddies, and we go up there one night.

Marian

You were like 14.

Jack

Yeah, 14. So I walk up to the door, tap on the door, and the little slide opens up. I said, "I know what this is! But I won't blow a whistle if you let us in!" (laughter)

They told me, "Junior, you get out of here!" (laughter) So that made me mad. I thought, well, with a lot of crime, they get rewards from the police department. And I said, "I know where there's a whore house. I'll tell you where it's at if I get a reward." But they wouldn't give me a reward, but I did blow the whistle. It was a huge whore house.

Marian

Yes, it was. They had it in the paper, the San Jose Times. The headline said: "House of ill repute found on Roddy Ranch." Dad was furious! He had them retract it the next day.

The Roddy ranch

Let's fast forward to 1973. Jimmy Roddy tells a story about his dad, John.

The Old Man and Tom Sondgroth were going to Elko, Nevada, to buy cattle. And they get to Winnemucca. And Tom said, "John, it's been a long drive. I'm a little parched. Do you want to stop and have a beer?"

And the Old Man says, "Now that's a hell of a good idea, a little beer would be grand. It's been a long ride from San Jose." So Tom kept passing by different bars. We could have stopped right in. He went to the middle of the town, took a left across traffic, and went down the road. There were a bunch of these funny little houses, there were.

"Now, I had a sneakin' suspicion, there were a bunch of them whore houses, but I wasn't quite sure, and so I walked right in, I did. There was a whole bunch of girls looking really horny with not too much clothes on. Can you imagine? A good Catholic Irish lad like myself in a whore house. So I sat down at the bar. I was still going to have my beer. But that wasn't the bad part. On the wall, behind the bar, at the house of ill repute. There was me two boys' pictures, autographed. You know, you're supposed to be proud of the bastards. Where do you find their pictures? At the whore house."

Never Dull!

JIMMY RODDY

Marian

Jim, tell the one about the car.

Jimmy

We were driving up the road, and we saw 100 feet of the fence down. Usually, people drove in one side, and then would drive out. But this guy, he got hung up. From the top of the ranch down to Alum Rock Park was about 3,000 feet. And there he was, hanging on the side of the cliff.

And the Old Man says, "We finally caught one of the dirty bastards." So we walked up a little closer. You could see where he backed up and pulled ahead. He was trying to commit suicide right off the hill. He couldn't back up anymore. He was really in trouble. And the Old Man bent down and looked in and said, "Oh, for pities' sake. Wake your arse up! What in the hell are you doing here?"

The guy says, "I lost my wife. I lost my job. I've been on drugs. Life is not worth living. I want to end it all."

The Old Man says, "Now lad, don't be a failure all yer' life. Take your foot off the brake."

Jack

That was true.

Marian

Didn't he start pushing the car, too?

Jimmy

Yeah. He got behind the car and started pushing. He said, "I'll help 'ya." Then the cops showed up. The only time in my life that I laid my hands on my dad was to stop him from pushing that car over the edge.

61

NEVER DULL!

Now let's rewind to 1953. John Roddy believed children should be seen and not heard. Jack was 16 and on his way to his full height of six-foot-five. Nancy was 15, and Marian was 13. They all went to the fair, and their dad said, "I have some business to do. Go away." In an unusual move, he gave them some money, and they scooted off to the carnival.

JIMMY (LEFT) AND
JACK AGE 17

The first ride they went on was called *The Barrel of Fun.* It was a giant spinning tube, eight feet tall by twenty feet long. Similar to the one in the closing scene of the movie Grease. Nancy would not go on the ride because she did not want to mess up her hair. Mom tells the following story.

THE RODDY RANCH

BARREL OF FUN - PHOTO CREDIT KRISTIE NIGHT

Marian

Nancy loved to look good. We slept in twin beds in the same room. Nancy would wash and set her hair once a week. To keep her hair perfect, she would wrap her hair in toilet paper each night. She would lay there like a statue! She did not move!

Jack was athletic and sprinted right through, he looped around again, and this time he spread his arms and legs like a starfish and braced himself in the spinning tube. I was behind him and crawled through on my hands and knees. I was a scrawny teenager and not athletic. I lost my footing and went halfway up, and then SPLAT. I kept trying to crawl. Around and around that stupid barrel went SPLAT! SPLAT! I was laughing so hard I peed my pants, and it left a spiral of pee in the tube. (laughter) The carnival ride operator had to shut it down, get a hose, and spray it out. (laughter)

Fifty years later, Mom was telling that story at a trail ride. Her friend said, "Oh no! Marian! Weren't you mortified?"

"Eh, not really. I didn't know anybody there. I wasn't embarrassed. I just kept moving forward."

That sums up my mom's attitude perfectly. Just keep moving forward.

It sounds like a fun childhood, doesn't it?, But there was a lot of alcohol, a lot of drama..My mom and her mother, Ann, had a rough time. When Mom and I would fight, right before sending me to my room, she would say, "There was no manual on how to be a good mother. I got no training."

I realize now she was doing her best. My mom and dad never really fought. Not because they didn't have any problems. Every couple in the history of the world has problems. They didn't fight because they did not know how to disagree effectively.

Mom thought that raised voices meant bloodshed. Dad didn't want anyone to be upset. As a result, they didn't talk about difficult issues. They had never had a fight because neither one told the other no.

One night, the word to solve the puzzle on Wheel of Fortune was passive-aggressive. I asked Mom and Dad, "What does that mean?"

They just grinned at each other.

What I learned from that was to talk about things. Face your problems head-on and learn to disagree because no one has a perfect life.

John was extremely tough on his kids. Mom told me she was always second-guessing the words and tone her dad used. Like when Nolan asked for her hand, and John said, "I thought I'd never get rid of her. Have at her."

Sometimes she thought she was overthinking everything and should not worry about it. Other times her self-confidence was destroyed.

There was no back-and-forth between Mom and her parents. John talked *at* the kids but didn't listen to what they said. When Mom cried or showed emotion, he told her to toughen up.

Marian

I remember I won San Jose Rodeo, and I tied Sammy Thurman, of all people; she was my hero. And I was riding Drifter, and my dad donated the buckle. So that night, I said to him, "Dad, we need to have another buckle because we tied."

He said, "No, you won't have another buckle. You'll just have a runoff. And whoever wins, wins."

And I said, "No, just give me the buckle." It was my first buckle, and luckily I beat her the next go-round. But he was not going to buy another buckle. He didn't care who it was.

NEVER DULL!

Grandpa had a lot of money. They were very wealthy. He could have easily afforded another buckle.

There is a saying that goes like this:

Spoil your kids, and you will raise your grandkids.

Raise your kids and you get to spoil your grandkids.

SAN JOSE BARREL RACING BUCKLE - 1963

Chapter 6

Unusual and Innovative

When Mom and Dad moved to Danville in 1964, Leslie Forman was one of his first clients. She and her husband had also just moved to a beautiful property next to the Mount Diablo State Park. It had miles and miles of horse trails.

For four years, Leslie had been a flight attendant for United Airlines before getting married. For a while, she was able to keep her marital status secret, but then she was outed and fired. Can you imagine?

In the 1960s, United was one of many airlines that barred married flight attendants from working. The airlines believed male business travelers would be lured to their airline by the pretty, single women serving as air hostesses. In 1986, the case went to the US Supreme Court. Among other things, the defense argued that "some of the stewardesses were husband-hunters. They never intended to make the job a career." The airlines argued that some women were using the airline, not the other way around. So, it made perfect sense to fire them if they got married.

NEVER DULL!

The plaintiffs won, and Leslie returned to flying for 17 more years.

While she was grounded, Leslie was looking for something to keep her busy and had memories of the strong bond she had with her horse while growing up in Ohio. Riding a horse again would be just what the doctor ordered. No medicine on the earth is as good as a horse. As Teddy Roosevelt said, "The outside of a horse is good for the inside of a man."

But it had been years and years since she had a horse and considered herself an absolute novice. She bought a horse named Amber. Leslie knew the horse was a she, but that was about it.

Dad came to her house to give Amber the once-over. He said, "My wife rides these trails all the time. You two would really get along."

He floated Amber's teeth, wormed her, and gave her shots. Leslie was startled when Dad put his arm all the way up Amber's fanny. Dad knitted his brow and tilted his head. He pulled out his arm and smiled as he removed the shoulder-high plastic glove. He told Leslie, "Congratulations! You're going to be a mother."

"What!"

Leslie's husband, Peter, became our dentist, and Leslie became Mom's best friend. That friendship would last over 60 years. Leslie still marvels at how Mom could talk her into anything. Mom loved fashion and convinced Leslie to become her business partner and open a women's boutique in Danville —more about the hysterical wholesale buying trip in a few chapters.

UNUSUAL AND INNOVATIVE

MARIAN AND LESLIE FORMAN - 2019

Mom was so ahead of the trends. She was a fashionista before that word was invented. Dad had to keep his clothes in another closet to allow room for her vast wardrobe of handmade cowboy shirts and pants—the more sparkly, the better. She had cowboy boots in white, black, green, blue, pink, and red, with matching cowboy hats in every color.

The barrels were painted differently at each rodeo, and she would color-coordinate her outfit to match. Her favorite was red and white at the Livermore Rodeo. The Madonna Inn Rodeo had pink barrels; she wore a pink hat, pink shirt, and pink boots.

At the Cow Palace one year, the barrels were red, white, and blue. She loved that! Then the Cow Palace switched to orange barrels, and that really ticked her off. She looked terrible in orange.

NEVER DULL!

MARIAN SHARP · San Luis Obispo, Ca · 74

MARIAN IN PINK TO MATCH THE BARRELS AT MADONNA INN RODEO - 1974 BRENDA ALLEN

Mom hated her natural hair color. Mousy Brown was just too boring. Even though she knew blonds had more fun, she wanted to be a redhead. To save money, she dyed her own hair. She didn't want the hair dye to get on her jammies, so she colored her hair while naked. She was typically very good at multitasking but got distracted and talked too long on the phone one day. She lost track of time and didn't hear the timer go off.

Unusual and Innovative

We lived out in the country, and the only phone in the house at the time was in the living room, in front of the plate glass window. She was yacking away on the phone while sitting naked on the fake leather couch. It was hot and her cheeks were sticking to the cushions, but that was the only place to sit. She completely lost track of time because the phone conversation was so entertaining.

The mailman came every day at 10 AM and surprised her when he knocked on the front door.

She yelled into the phone, "Oh, crap! Gotta go!" She stopped, dropped, and rolled, and crawled on her hands and knees to the bathroom. She took a hot shower and laughed at herself. After she dried off, she used the towel to wipe the fog off the mirror.

AGGHHHH! Her hair was fire engine red.

Wigs were popular then, and thankfully she had a large assortment.

That weekend was the Oakdale Rodeo. It had just rained, and the arena was a muddy mess, so she decided to take her horse, Sugar, because he was so sure-footed.

The rodeo announcer said, "Next up is Marian Sharp. The louder you cheer, the faster they run!" Mom cued Sugar perfectly, and he wrapped the first barrel. With explosive speed, he ran to the second barrel. The ground was slick. As he went around that barrel, Sugar slipped and almost fell. When he stumbled, he jerked the reins out of her hand. She grabbed the saddle horn with both hands. Her hat fell off, and took her wig with it. The announcer yelled, "Holy moly!" The horse was such an athlete. He got to his feet and kept running to the third barrel.

The announcer saw the wig and the hat in the mud. With alarm, he said, "Ladies and gentlemen, for your safety, remain in the stands! A rodent has attacked Marian's head and is still in the arena. Look at the blood on her head! It is bright red and she is holding on for dear life!"

Sugar turned the third barrel on his own. She got the reins back in her hands as they crossed the finish line. Everyone was looking at her with their mouths hanging open. She didn't cry or try to flee. She just laughed. She ruffled her hair and shrugged her shoulders. Her reaction is not what anyone expected from a woman who was so concerned about her looks. But her attitude was, "Shit happens. Nothing I can do about it."

The announcer saw Dad jump the fence and jog in to retrieve the wig. The announcer said, "To subdue this vicious animal, we have retained the services of world-renowned veterinarian Dr. Nolan Sharp." Dad started laughing and gave a thumbs-up.

The announcer said, "I'd be afraid if I were you, Doc. Do you have a tranquilizer? Are you armed? That thing is ferocious. Look what it did to your wife's head." When Dad got close, he pretended to shoot the rodent with his fingers. He holstered his 'gun,' picked up the wig, placed it on his head, and jogged back.

I am embarrassed to report that this would not be the last time my dad wore a wig. Actually, I am not embarrassed. I am proud of him. He knew exactly who he was, and so did my mom.

In the 1970s, streaking was all the rage. Once a month, there was a news story about someone who stripped off their clothes in San Francisco and ran thru city hall or streaked during the 49ers game.

Pat, the one who was with Mom the day she met my dad, was married to Don Flanigan and lived at the Twin Creeks Ranch. She and Mom were grousing about how Don and my dad needed to liven up and have some fun.

People would come to Pat and Don's place every Thursday afternoon to rope in the arena. Jack Sparrowk was not there that day, but his dad, Mr. Sparrowk, was. Heavy on the Mister. He was a strict Baptist and very conservative. Mr. Sparrowk dressed impeccably and wore a crisp white shirt every day. Most people were intimidated by him because he was so serious. He was a pillar of the community and the brains behind Alamo's first development. The words silly or immature would never be used to describe Mr. Sparrowk.

To loosen up their husbands and make them laugh, Mom and Pat had a bright idea. Large Monterey pine trees were on the arena's west side. They provide shade on hot summer afternoons. Mom and Pat stripped down to nothing but their socks. They hung their shirts, bras, and panties on the branches and stood on their jeans to avoid the star thistle.

Never Dull!

They hid behind the trees to wait for Don and my dad to ride back from the catch pen. They thought they timed it right and jumped out to surprise their husbands.

"Ta-Da!"

Oops, bad timing.

The person riding back from the catch pen was Mr. Sparrowk. He tipped his hat and politely said, "Good afternoon."

He rode back to the roping chute and pulled his horse to a stop near Don and my dad. Mr. Sparrowk looked straight ahead and dusted a spec of dirt off his shirt. He told them dryly, "You two should spend some time teaching your wives how to iron."

Don and my dad looked at each other perplexed.

Mr. Sparrowk looked at them, "Their birthday suits are wrinkled."

Sadly, this would not be the last time Mom did not have clothes on. You would think she would learn. Stay tuned.

I know you will have a hard time believing this, but there was someone who liked to talk on the phone more than my mom. Her sister Nancy could talk non stop and did not like to be interrupted. Sometimes Mom would set the phone down, go to the bathroom, do a load of laundry, get a cup of coffee, and come back, and Nancy would never know she was gone.

Things had improved financially, and now there were two phones in the house. Mom was in her bedroom looking out across the front lawn. The windows were wide open for cross ventilation because we didn't have air conditioning yet. The heat was making my mom cranky. She looked outside across the lawn and said, "I am not putting up with this anymore. Hold on a sec."

She set the baby-blue phone down on the waterbed, marched across the burnt-orange shag carpet, and pulled open the drawer of Dad's avocado-green nightstand. Nancy was still talking a mile a minute.

A gunshot rang out at close range.

Nancy shouted, "Mar! What happened? Mar! Talk to me!"

Mom picked up the phone and said nonchalantly, "Nan. I gotta go."

"Wait! What happened?"

"Oh, settle down!" Mom was irritated that her big sister was bossing her around, "It's no big deal. I shot that little bastard between the eyes."

"What! Who!"

"A gopher"

"Where!"

"He was tearing up my lawn. Dang it, I wasn't thinking. I put a hole in the screen."

"What? How!"

"I picked up the gun and shot him."

"You have a loaded gun in your dresser?"

"Of course. Don't you?"

Before Dad built the vet clinic in 1970, he operated on the lawn in front of our house on Lawrence Road. In the second picture, Dad is on a bucket, and I am in my onesie. You can't tell, but Mom is eight months pregnant with Brian.

Dad had a creative mind and lots of ideas. He was tired of bending over during surgery.

SURGERY ON THE FRONT LAWN

NOLAN, HEATHER, MARIAN - 1968

UNUSUAL AND INNOVATIVE

Dad was just starting his practice and was not picky about his clients. Money was tight and he had big plans. He would go on any call and go vet work for anyone. He was not picky. He figured, *You've got to start somewhere.* He did not feel entitled just because he had a few letters behind his name.

One of his clients had six cows and one bull. This was his herd. He called himself a cattleman, but this was his hobby. In real life, he owned an auto body repair shop.

Dad went out to the guy's place to preg-check the cows. Unfortunately, the guy didn't have a chute. Part of the challenge was that Dad would rope the cows, the man would hold the cows still by twitching their nose, and Dad would do a preg-check. Luckily most of the cows were pretty gentle, and it was a small pen.

While the two of them were chasing the cows around, they made small talk. The man said he was remodeling his auto body shop and installing a new hydraulic car lift. Dad asked if he could have the old one.

The man said, "I thought I'd never get rid of it. Sure, have at her." Dad grinned because those were the exact words his father-in-law had used. And that turned out pretty good. This would too.

Dad was able to preg-check five out of six cows, but the last one was too hard to catch. The boards on the fence were old and falling down, and Dad could picture himself running down Highland Road, trying to catch this cow after she jumped out of the pen. The man stood in front of the weak spot in the fence and told Dad to give it one more try.

Never Dull!

The cow ran around that pen like she was at the Kentucky Derby. Dad was winded and put his hands on his knees. He said, "I don't need to catch her. I can tell just by looking at her that she's pregnant. She has that embarrassed look in her eye like she's been naughty."

"Do you think you can have a look at my daughter then?"

"No, I only specialize in hoofed animals."

The man sighed, "All right then. Only one of them better be pregnant, and I sure hope it's the cow. Even though you didn't catch the cow, I'll still give you the car lift. What are you going to do with it?"

Dad explained his idea of creating an operating table for a 1,100-pound horse. He said many horses get injured when they wake up from surgery, so he would build an operating room with padded floors and padded walls.

Dad said, "I have another client that has a music store. He is going to get me four-by-eight sheets of three-inch foam. Another client is an engineer for Dow Chemical. He's got a rubberized paint product. It goes on a quarter-inch thick and creates a flexible seal. He will give me fifty gallons of it because the color is Emerald Green, and the customer wanted Army Green."

The man asked, "Huh, what did they use that for?"

"I don't know. I suspect it was for the Military. Probably some secret stuff. Anyway, when the table is stowed, it will go all the way down in the ground and be flush with the floor. Before the horse comes in, I will lift the table up with hydraulics and then tilt it 90 degrees perpendicular to the floor. The horse will walk in right next to the table. The table will have D-rings on it and belly bands. I'll give the horse a mild tranquilizer, put the belly bands on, give the horse a stronger sedative to knock him out, and tilt the table back parallel to the ground and operate. Then I can do surgery standing up and have good lighting."

The guy nodded, "How will you get the table to tilt 90 degrees?"

Dad shrugged, "Can't be that hard. Anything is possible. I'll figure it out. When I finish the surgery, I will lower the table so it is flush with the floor again. I made a padded helmet for horses. I'll put that on, close the door, and turn the lights out. The horse will have a nice little nap and wake up peacefully."

"Huh, sounds like it will work. Has anybody done this before?"

"Nope! Universities have something similar, but nothing like this. This will be the first one in private practice."

Dad hobbled together this Rube Goldberg contraption so that he could do surgery standing up.

His motto was, *Think outside the box. Anything is possible.*

Never Dull!

BRIAN ON THE OPERATING TABLE
WITH DAD - 1970

Chapter 7

KIDS SAY THE DARNDEST THINGS

On Mom's 75th birthday, she showed me a card she'd received. It said, *When people tell you to enjoy them while they're young, they don't mean your children. They mean your hips and knees.*

Then, she told me about when I was little. She said, "Little kids should come with warning labels. They are like parrots. They repeat everything they hear."

When I was four, my dad drove our family to Los Altos and picked up his mom and sister for church on Easter Sunday. Dad was driving, and Mom was in front, holding Brian. This was way before car seats. Gram and Sylvia were in the back, with me in the middle. Mom had me dressed up like a little doll. I wore a handmade dress with white gloves, white tights, and patent leather shoes. I was her life-size Barbie. Gram and Sylvia were telling me how adorable I was.

Dad bragged to Gram that I was his little helper and went everywhere with him.

Mom said, "Heather wants to be just like her dad."

Never Dull!

Awwww. Isn't that sweet?

As we drove south on El Camino Real, our pleasant Sunday morning was ruined by a tailgater. Dad looked in the rearview mirror and tightened his grip on the wheel. The car honked, flashed its lights, and then zipped around our car. Dad had to slam on the brakes.

From the back seat, I yelled, "Shit! You see that some bitch!"

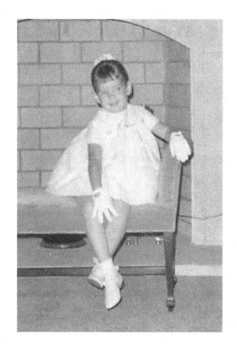

1971

KIDS SAY THE DARNEDEST THINGS

Mom usually brought a babysitter with her to the rodeos. But Tammy was unavailable on that infamous day. I was four-and-a-half years old and riding double in front of my mom. She was warming up her horse to run at the Livermore Rodeo. Mom was nervous that the barrel racing would start before my dad came back from the rotary tent.

She spied her brother Jack pulling into the rodeo grounds in his gold Oldsmobile and two-horse trailer. My pigtails bounced, and I giggled as she trotted her horse over to his car. When he got out of his car, she lifted me off the saddle and handed me to him.

"Hey, Sugar! Give me somethin' sweet." He held me on his hip, and I gave him a big smack, and he gave me a whisker burn.

Mom said, "Can you watch Heather? Just until Nolan gets back."

Jack said, "Where's Nolan?"

NEVER DULL!

I piped up, "Dads at the twirly thingy. He is throwing up waffles."

Mom sighed, "What she means is . . .he is at the Rotary booth flipping pancakes. I'll be twenty minutes tops! I swear." She squished her red cowboy hat down and trotted towards the arena.

Jack hollered, "You owe me! I'll get you back for this!"

The barrels at Livermore Rodeo were red and white. She liked to be color-coordinated at every event she went to. As she got further away, he yelled, "You look like a candy cane!"

Jack took me to the concession stand and bought me an ice cream. While we sat in the stands, I was swinging my legs, eating my ice cream, and yammering just like little girls do.

Sounds like a sweet moment between a little girl and her uncle, right?

Jack looked at his watch, "Where's your dad?"

I said, "I don't know. Maybe he's having a heart attack."

"What? Why would you say a crazy thing like that?"

I told him all sorts of very private details about my dear old Dad. He tried to suppress a smile and pumped me for more information.

When I finished, he soberly said, "Oh dear, that sounds serious. If I get you another ice cream, do you think you can tell that story again?"

"Ummm hmm," I nodded eagerly. I would do anything for my uncle.

"You're a good girl." He kissed me on the top of my head and said, "Let's go get you another ice cream."

MARIAN IN RED AND WHITE TO
MATCH THE BARRELS AT
LIVERMORE -FOXIE PHOTO

That evening after the rodeo, a hospitality tent was set up for all the cowboys. There would be a Santa Maria-Style BBQ and a dance after. The bar was packed when Mom and Dad came in with me. When I saw Jack at the bar, I jumped up and down. He spotted us and waved us over. When we got close, I broke away and ran toward my uncle. He scooped me up and set me on the bar. "Bartender! Get my favorite girl a Shirley Temple!"

Oh! I was in Heaven.

NEVER DULL!

"So Heather," Jack signaled the crowd to be quiet and gather around. "Tell me again what we talked about this morning. I'm worried about your dad."

I took a deep breath, "Sometimes, I think he's having a heart attack."

"Really? Can you tell me the noises he makes?"

I happily obliged and even included the grunting.

Jack said, "Sweetheart, it's loud in here. Can you speak up?"

I dialed up my volume to max. Everyone at the bar fell silent and snapped their heads to see this little girl on the bar relaying the sounds she heard. It sounded like a porno. Everyone laughed hysterically, including my parents. Mom tried to put her hand over Jack's mouth, but with his long arms, he held her back.

"And does your Mommy make noises too?"

"Sometimes she does."

Jack was concerned. He said, "Maybe she is asleep?"

"I try to get in, but the door is locked. I bang and bang. I try to get her to wake up. But she doesn't hear me."

I got a round of applause from the bar and a big hug from my uncle. He said, "That's the most precious thing I have ever heard. Forget the ice cream. I am going to buy you a pony!"

Chapter 8

THE RODEO YEARS

In 1972, Jack Roddy, Jack Sparrowk, and Bob Cook joined forces to create RSC, the Rodeo Stock Contracting Company.

The initials were based on their last names. The plan was hatched at a bar after a rodeo and the brand was drawn on the back of a napkin.

JACK RODDY, BOB COOK AND JACK SPARROWK - 1972

RSC BRAND

NEVER DULL!

They knew a lot about rodeos and how they should be run. And like every cowboy, they deeply respected and loved the animals they competed against.

Jack Sparrowk and Jack Roddy went to school at Cal Poly together. Jack Roddy would become the World Champion Steer Wrestler in 1966 and 1968. Jack Sparrowk went on to become the President of CattleFax and a board member at the National Cowboy and Western Heritage Museum in Oklahoma City.

The trajectory of my life would change because of Bob Cook, but you will have to wait a few chapters to find out why.

JACK SPARROWK AND JACK
RODDY - 1972

THE RODEO YEARS

The following is transcribed from Jack Sparrowk:

Years ago, Bob Cook called me up and told me that he was up in the Bulldogging in Sacramento and asked me if I would ride up to the rodeo with him that night because I wasn't up. So we're riding up there, and about that time the PRCA was trying to get a new stock contractor on the West Coast because Cotton Rosser was just spread too thin. He was the only stock contractor on the west coast, and he was putting on more rodeos than he had the right kind of stock for. And Jack Roddy was a mover and shaker in the rodeo business. So Cook tells me, he says, "Hey, Jack Roddy and I want to get in the rodeo business. But Jack Roddy says the only way he'll get in it is if Jack Sparrowk is our partner."

Well, I was flattered by that comment from Jack Roddy. So I told Cook to count me in, that I'd be a partner. About six months later, Jack Roddy and I were sitting around talking, and Jack says, "You know," he said, "I would have never gotten in the rodeo business but Bob Cook told me that he and Jack Sparrowk wanted to get in the rodeo business. And Jack Sparrowk said the only way he would get in it is if Jack Roddy was our partner." So bottom line is, Cook told Jack Roddy and myself both the same story and we ended up in the rodeo business together.

So after we'd been in the rodeo business several years we were getting a little disenchanted with it because I was real busy in the cattle business and

NEVER DULL!

Jack Roddy was real busy with his bars and his other enterprises. And the rodeo deal was taking a lot of work and wasn't making any money. So Jack Roddy was single at the time. And we put the rodeo on in Bishop, California. And as soon as the rodeo was over we drove all night to Lancaster, California, to put on the rodeo there the next day.

Well, Jack had flown some beauty queen. I think she'd been in the Miss America contest or something. He had flown her in to meet him at Lancaster and somebody had picked her up at the airport and drove her out to the rodeo grounds. And, of course, Lancaster was hotter than the devil and she's sitting in Jack's Cadillac with the air conditioner running and Jack Roddy and myself and Bob Tallman are working our tails off putting up the portable arena. We no sooner get the arena put up and it's time to saddle the pickup horses. And there's Miss America still sitting in the Cadillac with the air conditioner on.

So Jack Roddy and myself, we jump on our horses and picked up. The rodeo was over and we're feeding the stock. Bob Cook told us to go feed the stock. So here we are out there, 100 degrees. Miss America is in the car with the air conditioner on and we're busting our tail off. Cook comes walking by and he was upset with Jack Roddy about something, and he reads Jack Roddy the riot act. And Jack looked at me, and I looked at him, and we both looked at

Miss America, and Roddy and I decided maybe it was time for us to exit the rodeo business.

That's a true story. And I kid Jack about that all the time when I see him. I don't know what kind of a beauty queen she was, but she was a knockout. Of course, at that time, Jack was the most eligible bachelor around. Anyway, that's the way we got in the rodeo business, and that's when we decided that we probably needed to do something different.

In 1972, a well-known stock contractor, Bob Barmby, sold his second string rodeo bucking stock to RSC, including the bucking bull Oscar.

In the first five years that RSC owned Oscar, over 100 bull riders tried and failed to get a qualified ride. To incentivize the riders, RSC offered a bronze statue of Oscar to the first rider to make a qualified ride on him. I don't know who won that bronze, but I do know that eight-time world champion bull rider Don Gay marked a 97-point ride on Oscar. At the time, that was the highest scored ride ever, just 3 points short of a perfect score.

Oscar bucked over 300 times in his lifetime, and only eight cowboys rode him for the full eight seconds.

In 1979, the year Oscar retired, he was inducted into the Pro Rodeo Hall of Fame. Only seven bulls have ever been inducted. He lived out the

OSCAR THE BULL - 1972

rest of his life as a living exhibit at the ProRodeo Hall of Fame in Colorado Springs.

But before he retired, Oscar made his film debut in a Disney film called The Great American Cowboy. That film won the 1974 Academy Award for Best Documentary. The movie is available on YouTube and cowboybookworm.com.

At the end of the movie, there is a scene where Larry Mahan rides Oscar in an empty rodeo arena with no one around to watch. The date of the filming was supposed to be kept a secret, but one cowboy told two friends, and they told two friends, and so on.

Jimmy Roddy was there and described that day.

In the movie, The Great American Cowboy, Larry Mahan got on the bull, Oscar, and nobody was supposed to be in the stands at Lake Comanche Rodeo. The only people supposed to be there was, Larry Mahan, myself, Cook, and nobody else. Well, word got out there were 2,000 people there.

LARRY MAHAN ON OSCAR, JIMMY RODDY WATCHING - 1973

The Old Man asked Dominic, "Now Dominic, where do you think the best place to watch this Mahan and this Oscar is?"

And Dominic thinks a minute and says, "Mr. Roddy," he says, "see the spot three feet out in front of the shoot? That would be the best place."

And the Old Man says, "Now Dominic, where do you think the second-best place is?"(laughter)

When I was 11, I went to the Oakdale Rodeo with my mom. After her run, she was going to drive me four hours to my friend Jamie Capp's house. Jamie's mom is Edie Capps, the same one from Chapter One with the shiney hineys.

At the rodeo, Mom saw John W and JoAnn Jones and asked if they could give me a ride since San Ardo was on their way home, and it would save her a trip. After all, she was very busy.

John W was the very same one that cut off Mom's ponytail. He had such a dry sense of humor and a quick wit. If he were alive today, I am sure he would offend people. And when I say *people,* I mean snowflakes. I believe, just as Mom did, you cannot take things personally, and you cannot be easily offended, just like water off a duck's back. If you want to play with the big dogs, you have to have a thick skin.

John W was driving his blue Ford pickup pulling a red two-horse trailer down the highway near Coalinga. It wasn't quite the middle of nowhere, but you could see it from there. John W had been making fun of me the whole way down. JoAnn was telling him to be nice to me, but I loved it.

Never Dull!

I was sitting in the center of the truck when suddenly, the truck lurched hard to the left. The next thing you know, a spinning tire passed us and bounced across the other lane of oncoming traffic.

John W elbowed me, "Heather! Fetch!" The truck skidded to a stop. John looked over at me and said, "Now what?" I shrugged, he shrugged, and JoAnn hit her forehead with her palm.

The good news was that no other cars were coming for the tire to run into. The bad news was that there would be no cars for over one hour.

It was scorching hot, and we were stranded. The entire axle had come off, and it was a Sunday. We unloaded horses out of the burning trailer. John W looked across the desert at the maximum security prison. He asked JoAnn, "I wonder if we could trade Heather for a ride to town?"

"John!" JoAnn scolded him.

"You're right. I'd just trade her for a glass of water."

Because he teased me, I knew he liked me.

God was looking out for us. A van passed us, slowed down, and turned around. The driver got out and asked how he could help.

There was no air conditioning in the van and a herd of kids in matching clothes got out. The boys had on straw hats, and the girls had on bonnets. Next came a very pregnant woman in a bonnet. She was rubbing her back and cradling her tummy. JoAnn made small talk with her, and I played with the kids.

THE RODEO YEARS

The driver and John looked at the axle. The man tipped his flat brimmed hat back and wiped his brow. There was a lot of head shaking and sucking of teeth. The man said, "We have horses. I'll go get the trailer. Your horses can stay at our place while I take you to get your tire fixed."

What a nice guy! He dropped his family off at his farm and returned with his horse trailer. We loaded the horses and went back to his place. Just as we got out of the van, the tallest kid came running around the corner of the barn, yelling, "She's having a baby! She's having a baby!"

JoAnn's eyes widened, and John W shrugged, "This is an exciting day."

"Come quick!" the boy yelled. "Mother told me to get you! Hurry!" He grabbed John W's hand and pulled him forward. John W reluctantly stumbled after the kid and looked over his shoulder at JoAnn. Now it was her turn to shrug, and we followed them around the corner of the barn. We didn't have to go far to find them. JoAnn and I stood on either side of John W.

It wasn't the mom--it was their mare! The entire family anxiously stood around a mare who was clearly in labor. The mom said, "It's Sunday. The vet's at church."

"You're in luck!" John W grabbed me by the shoulders and thrust me forward. "Heather knows exactly what to do. Her dad is a vet." I spun around and glared at him with big eyes. He chuckled and pointed at the mare. "Go for it!"

I was eleven years old. I tentatively walked up to the mare. I put my hand on her butt and softly said, "Ummm. OK, sweetie. Lie down." Boom. She lay down.

NEVER DULL!

I thought, *Hmmm, this is easy.* I moved around to her head and stroked her neck. I was more confident and said, "OK, sweetie . . . push."

The mare was twenty years old and probably had 15 babies over her lifetime. Two pushes—boom! Out came a colt. I felt the blood pumping through the umbilical cord while the mare rested. When the pumping stopped, I said, "OK, sweetie . . . You can stand up now." Boom! She stood up.

The force of her standing up broke the umbilical cord. The mare licked the colt. He stood up and started nursing immediately.

The whole family cheered. The parents were crying and the kids were jumping up and down. The woman said, "God puts the right people in your path at the right time."

I said, "The mare could have done this all by herself. She didn't need me. You were the ones that saved us. We are thanking God for you."

HEATHER WITH A NEWBORN COLT
- 1974

Chapter 8 ½

THE BIG PICTURE

This chapter was inserted after the book was finished. I could have added it to the end, but it is most appropriate here because of the people that I talked with. I will tell you why it happened in a few paragraphs. I am getting a glimpse of the big picture. It was definitely a God thing.

I interviewed many people for this book. When I called Bill McCulloch, who you will read about much later in Chapter 18 in a story completely unrelated to rodeo. I was surprised to learn that Bill knew my uncle in the 1970s. He told me, "Your family was always so nice to me -your uncle Jack in particular. I will never forget that. Many years ago, I was the rodeo coach at Fresno State. I was a nobody and your uncle was a big deal. He cut a wide swath and had many friends who were a lot more important than me. He would always take the time to help me and talk to the kids on the rodeo team. He inspired them to achieve their dreams."

NEVER DULL!

Emmy Award winner Clint Pulver is quoted as saying, "There is a difference between being the best in the world and being the best for the world."

I am proud to say Jack was both.

My parents understood what was important. They knew that you were not going to take your gold buckles with you to Heaven. God doesn't care about buckles, awards, or how much money you have. He cares about who you are inside.

What I learned from my family and all the other legends in this book was to treat everyone equally. Be kind to everyone and do not be impressed by wealth. Judge a person by what is in their heart, not their wallet. It all started with my Grandpa Roddy and this quote from Abe Lincoln, "God must have loved the plain people because he made so many of them."

After I wrote this book, I thought, *I know how Bill feels. I am a nobody too. I have this great story to tell. I am not in the same circles as my parents anymore. I have no contacts, no clout.*

I knew I needed someone influential to endorse this book. Someone that had a platform and already had a relationship with the audience I wanted to reach. But I felt it was impossible because the book's publication date was already set, and there wasn't enough time for me to find someone.

I thought *I am just going to trust God. My mom said everything will work out. It always does. If the book only sells a few copies and one person's life gets touched by these stories, it will all be worth it.*

THE BIG PICTURE

A week before this book was to be published, there was a technical problem and the date would have to be pushed back a few weeks.

What!

But I had worked so hard and I had overcome roadblock after roadblock to meet the deadline.

I was so upset. I was sitting in church and supposed to be paying attention to the sermon but my mind was wandering. I was feeling sorry for myself and lamenting about my troubles.

Then I started talking to myself in my head, *Heather! Snap out of it! This is not a big deal. You have faced bigger problems than this before. Quit your whinin'.*

That's a clue. That's how you know when you are nuts. You start having conversations with yourself and you argue back. I ignored the voice in my head and decided, *What will be, will be. Don't worry, be happy.*

Then the idea popped into my head (I wonder where that came from? Thank you, God). I thought, *Since the book is delayed, I have time now that I didn't have before. I should shoot for the stars and ask the biggest names I can think of for an endorsement.*

My parents told me, "It never hurts to ask. He/she can always say no, but you won't know until you try."

I went home and wrote a letter the names that popped into my head, Bob Tallman and Pat Parelli.

I had been twenty-five years since the last time I talked with Bob Tallman at a rodeo for a whopping five minutes, and before that, it was over twenty years since I saw him, but he was always so nice to me. I had never met Pat Parelli, but I knew he and Dad were on the same wavelength and knew each other way back when, something like 40 or 45 years ago.

Bob Tallman has won the PRCA Rodeo Announcer of the Year 13 times and has been inducted into 15 Halls of Fame. Pat Parelli coined the term Natural Horsemanship and his program is taught in 76 countries. Both of them are extremely busy and certainly don't have time to do a favor for a nobody like me.

Because of my parents, both Bob and Pat called me back and without any hesitation, they said they would help me in any way they could.

I deeply appreciate them telling their story and now I get to share it with you.

Bob tells the story of how he got his start:

I attribute my success to people that helped mold my life and have impacted it in so many ways; Uncle Jack Roddy, Jack Sparrowk, the cowboy hero, and Bob Cook took me in when nobody else would hire me. Marian Sharp took me and my family in. And my *Pad-na*, Nolan Sharp, that's what he called me, *Pad-na*. We were team-roping partners.

Of course, there are many other people that helped me become successful. But they were the reason for my start. I was just a kid from Winnemucca, Nevada who didn't have a pot to piss in and wasn't even worried about what window I was gonna throw it out.

THE BIG PICTURE

It all started on February 3rd, 1972, when I moved to Clements, California, in a half-ton blue Ford pickup with a camper on the back.

My wife Kristen stayed at home and had a job so we could pay the bills. The people we met took us under their wing, introduced us to their circle of champions, and then they championed me. Nolan and Marian were unbelievable. So kind to us. I remember parking our camper at their house and plugging it into the barn. I'd go on veterinary calls with Dr. Sharp and roll beer kegs into the longest bar in the world in San Francisco for Grandpa John Roddy and Jack Roddy.

After Nicole, our daughter, was born, we would leave her with a diaper bag with Aunt Marian and she would keep her 2,3,4 days at a time while we tried to make our mark on the world. I got my start as a rodeo announcer because of the legends in this book. I can't begin to tell you how important my relationship with Jack Sparrowk was. He lobbied for me when Bob Cook and Jack Roddy said, "I don't know about this skinny, long-haired kid from Nevada."

Jack Sparrowk said, "He's a cowboy. I trust him."

This was a God wink before it was even a term we use today. I was about 23 years old and a cowboy from Nevada. I drove a truck for the RSC Rodeo Company. I built arenas and took care of the stock as well. Because I was five years older than my buddy,

BOB TALLMAN AND BOB COOK

Pat Parelli, who is still a great friend today, I drove the trucks and hauled the livestock. Pat would hose 'em out.

We were hauling rodeo stock to Clovis, California for the Fresno State College Rodeo and the announcer couldn't get there. At the last minute, Cook yelled at me and said, "Hey, you're a little wild and completely crazy, but I know you're not afraid.

Put on a clean shirt. Entertain us. Go announce the rodeo."

As I mentioned a moment ago. I called Nolan my partner because I rode his horses, his saddles and used his ropes. I could rope pretty good, I must have been impressive enough that Nolan said, Let's go enter.

He probably paid all the entry fees. And if we won, he let me keep my part of the winnings. Whether I turned two or ten steers for him, whether he roped one foot or two, we were partners and we had fun.

As they say, it's not about the destination. It's about the journey and who helped you travel on this road.

You know, folks, we came from humble beginnings and are now successful. My voice is a gift from God and I don't forget where my riches came from. We were blessed by knowing the people that you'll read about in this book, and now we're able to pay it forward and bless others.

Kristen and I have taken care of others in the rodeo industry; cowboys, bullfighters, clowns, ropers, it didn't matter. Anyone who didn't have family at Christmas, New Year's, Easter or Thanksgiving. Our table always has room for one of those that might be struggling at the moment.

NEVER DULL!

> Nolan and Marian treated us like family. And you know, it's the kindness and the trust that we were given that we now can extend to others.

Wow. That is so beautiful. I want that written on my tombstone.

That is a great illustration of dropping a pebble in a lake and having no idea of the ripple effect that will occur and who will be affected by your actions. Those ripples will create waves, and the next thing you know there is a tsunami.

My parents and the other legends helped Bob and his family because it was the right thing to do. They weren't nice because they were trying to work an angle to make themselves look better.

And because of my parent's kindness, people that Mom and Dad would never ever meet, like the cowboys sitting at Tallman's table during the holidays, are the ones that are benefiting. It is a beautiful thing. And my parents never knew that happened. Years from now, they will still be affecting other people. We all will. Good and bad.

When we die, the big picture will be revealed to us, as Dad said, "El Photo Grande," and we will be able to connect the dots. But until then, we may not know how our kindness affects others. We should just keep doing what we are doing. You might not be rewarded immediately, but you will be rewarded in Heaven.

I admit I am fearful. I am worried about the future of this country. I watch the news and I am depressed about where we are headed. Things are bad. I wonder if the ship is taking on too much water and we are going to sink. Or will we be able to turn things around and we can right the ship?

When I get worried, I remember what Mother Teresa once said; "I alone cannot change the world, but I can cast a stone across the waters to create many ripples."

I have to have faith that our pebbles will create a tsunami that will right the ship. The pendulum is going to swing back.

Bob Tallman mentioned his friend Pat Parelli. You will hear from Pat next about the influences and the mentors in his life. He went from hosing out a cattle truck to becoming a Bronc rider to having an international following but he never forgot where he came from and how he got his start.

Pat says this about Bob Tallman:

When I was 17 and Bob is, I believe five years older than me. We worked for R S C - Rodeo Stock Contractors, which was actually based on their last names: Roddy, Sparrowk, and Cook. Bob Tallman was the truck driver, and I was the kid that cleaned out the truck and opened chutes and, you know, did all the go-fer stuff. One day, the announcer didn't show up and Bob Cook hollers at him, "Bob Tallman, you got a big mouth! Get your butt up here and get on the microphone."

So that was the start of it. RSC started getting pro rodeos and I rode Broncs and Bob Tallman called me the Italian stallion. So we had a lot of fun times together.

NEVER DULL!

Bob Tallman is the greatest Rodeo announcer of all time. He enhanced everything that happened, like the old saying that music is nothing but silence between the notes. He knew when not to say something. He never got in the way of the action. That's why he's the greatest.

Pat Parelli talks about how he got his start, how critical influence is and the importance of setting goals:

My parents lived in Pleasanton on Happy Valley Road and my grandparents lived in Livermore off Vallecitos Road. In those days, I was hungry for any kind of knowledge and in that area there were great saddle bronc riders and bareback riders. And, Rowell Saddlery, they made the first bulldogging and calf roping saddles with a low cantle and all this stuff was going on. And Livermore, at one time was the rodeo cowboy capital of the world, and then it became Oakdale. There was so much action going on. I'd watched Doctor Billy Linfoot do wild horse taming at Reed's auction in Hayward. And that's what inspired me to want to become a person that could tame wild horses.

When I was 16, I was at the Cow Palace and saw John Edwards ride Cheyenne, one of the most famous bucking horses at the time. And I go, that's it. That's what I'm gonna be. And so even just the Cow Palace itself being an influence, we went in 4H and FFA, we went over for almost every single performance for two weeks, every year since I was ten years old and seeing all of these, you know, wonderful things, not just the rodeo, but the horse shows and all the different kinds of horses. All the English horses and hackney ponies and all the different breeds. I could only imagine trying to be one of those guys that got to do all that special stuff, you know, reach those heights.

At that time, between Santa Rosa and Salinas or Santa Barbara and Oakdale to San Francisco. That was the Vaquero Center. That's where all of that tradition came from.

The other day, somebody gave me these Western Horsemen Magazines dated 1943 and 1944; it was during the war, but it was in Alamo, that was where the headquarters was. And so the Western Horseman Magazine was actually Bay Area Magazine at first. The East Bay area was really the epicenter for great Western horsemanship.

And there was even a guy named Merle Lacy, and he had Arabians and I saw him playing with those Arabian stallions at Liberty and which was another inspiration that caused me to want to get horses to do things, even without a halter, or a bridle or saddle on.

I've told a lot of people I was born on Saint Patrick's Day and even though I'm Italian, it's the luck of the Irish because of where I was born and the influence of that era.

NEVER DULL!

I don't think a lot of people realize how important environmental influences and inspiration can be to somebody. We were in a special place: the Salinas Rodeo, the Livermore Rodeo, and the Hayward Rodeo.

Jack Roddy was still bulldogging back then. And his brother Jimmy was too. They had their ranch over there in San Jose below Mount Hamilton. And the area was infested with great inspiration, great riders and I was just lucky to be in the right place at the right time.

I took ambition pills every morning and wanted to learn everything from everybody I could and all those guys. And so it was just the perfect, it was the perfect storm for me.

I've always been interested in training animals. I trained my 4H steer, my sheep, my pig, I always fiddled around with the chickens and my dogs, I always taught him every trick in the world.

So when I started to rodeo, I started hanging around with the rodeo clowns. I started asking them, how do you get that horse or a donkey to do things?

Dale Woodard was one of my best friends. Dale had a pig one time called White Rock because Red Rock was a famous bull at the time. He had this white pig and trained that pig to do all these amazing things.

So I was really interested in that. Some of them had chimpanzees in their act, roosters and all that kind of stuff, I would always hang around the specialty acts and find out how they did that.

Wherever I was, if I heard there was a really good horseman, some old guy, I would find a way to get there.

The following picture is of Pat Parelli on the Bucking horse named Mr. Smith. He would later be known as Smith and Velvet because the Canadian whiskey, Black Velvet, was launching one of the first brand recognition advertising campaigns. Now that is all the rage, but they were one of the first.

The horse was inducted into the Pro Rodeo Hall of Fame in 2017. The following is from their website:

Bareback horse Smith & Velvet was the definition of a late bloomer.

The horse, which was honored as the PRCA's top bareback horse four times (1977, as Mr. Smith, and then 1979-80 and 1982, as Smith & Velvet), didn't become an award-winning bucker until he was into his 20s.

When owner Bobby Christensen first started bucking the horse, Smith & Velvet would be good for five or six seconds, and then he would spin and stop.

A lot of people told Christensen to get rid of the horse and that it would never reach its full potential. Instead, Christensen stayed the course and turned Smith & Velvet out for a few years.

The horse's comeback tour was complete when Christensen entered him in Oakdale, Calif., in the late 1970s, and he bucked off World Champion Jack Ward. From then on, Christensen knew he had a good horse, and the animal's career took off.

PAT PARELLI ON MR.
SMITH 1977

Smith & Velvet also faced five-time World Champion Joe Alexander – one of the greatest bareback riders of all-time – six times in his career, with man and beast each gaining the upper hand three times.

Bobby Christianson stuck with the horse and did not give up. That horse shows us all the value in believing *You are never too old.*

Today Pat Parelli is 69 years old and rides horses eight hours a day. More proof that age is just a number.

Pat started giving clinics in 1982, was one of the first horsemen to have a clinic to teach people how to understand what the horse was trying to tell us. They were five days long and cost $300 to bring your horse and $25 to watch. Five days! Five dollars a day.

Don't you wish we could go back in time? I wish we could for many reasons, but that is a whole other story.

I've got to take a little pause here and share with you how bizarre these last few days of my life have been. God's fingerprints are all over this. I feel like I am getting a peak at the big picture and connecting the dots.

As a kid, I knew Bob Tallman, but I had never met Pat Parelli. I did not know that Pat worked for RSC. I did not know he was friends with Bob. He was just a guy that I saw in magazines, but I knew that Pat and my Dad had worked on the same horses.

It wasn't until after Mom died that I realized Mom knew Tootie Bland.

The Rodeo world is small, but it's not that small.

NEVER DULL!

In the 1960s, Mom and Tootie Barrel Raced together and became friends. If it's even possible, Tootie's outfits were more glitzy and spectacular than Mom's. I bet the costume department for the movie *The Electric Horseman* got their ideas from these two.

All her life, Tootie had a desire to make the lives of horses better. Horses had given her so much and she wanted to give back. She knew the partnership between horse and human was stronger if it was based on trust rather than fear.

She had an idea, a dream really, to use entertainment as a vehicle to show the world what true horsemanship really is. She believed that through education, she could change people's minds.

Her idea was a televised competition between three horse trainers, who would each choose an untouched, unbroke three-year-old horse from a remuda (group of horses) from the historic 6666 Ranch and ride through an obstacle course on the third round of working with the horse. The competitors would wear a wireless mic to tell the audience what they were thinking. And more importantly, teach how to read a horse so the audience could understand what the horse was trying to communicate.

The audience would be part of the journey, from the selection of the horse to the final competition, and learn that horses will respond much faster to a whisper rather than a shout.

This was the complete opposite of an 8-second ride on a Bronc at a rodeo.

Old-timers told Tootie it couldn't be done.

The competitors would be judged on things like:

• Catching & Haltering, Saddling and Groundwork

• The competitor's demeanor and ability to build the colt's confidence.

• The competitor's ability to adjust to the colt's needs and build a solid foundation.

People told Tootie she had a nice idea but it would never work. They said, "No one is going to pay to watch that. And giving a horse trainer only three sessions are not long enough. There is no way. Just give up. It's not gonna happen."

The experts were wrong. This year Road to the Horse celebrated twenty years of sold-out crowds and the winner receives $100,000.

After Mom died, Tootie told me:

"There is no telling how many, many years your Mom and I have been friends. She was one of those friends who was always in your corner. I do miss her and all those wonderful years we experienced together. When I started Road to the Horse, most people considered it an "impossible endeavor."

Your Mom and I talked about the positives and negatives... and in the end ... she thought it was worth the effort and challenge. I always remember her in that special way of a friend that would give you the truth and the right word at the right time."

NEVER DULL!

Tootie changed many horses' lives, and Mom contributed to that by encouraging her to pursue her dreams. Mom thought anything was possible if you were willing to work hard.

It makes me so happy. It proves to all of us that we just don't know the power an encouraging word will have.

Mom was also known for telling the truth. She would not tell you what you wanted to hear. She would tell it like it is. If people were offended, well, that was just too bad. She loved the saying, "Suck it up, Buttercup."

Fast forward back to the present day. When I was stressed because of the delays associated with publishing this book, I could hear my mom's voice in my head saying, "Chill out Heather, everything will work out, it always does."

The book finally came together and at 8:03 AM today, I got an email that it was all systems go. Whoo-hooo! I did a happy dance in my kitchen. *Phew, it's finally over, now I can work on something else.*

Because I had been putting out fires elsewhere, I had put everything else on the back burner. In two weeks, I am going to be the keynote speaker at the Christian women's retreat called Horsewomen by Grace at a dude ranch called the Triangle C Ranch owned by Chris Cox. Last year, women came from ten states and during the four-day trail ride, three women were baptized in the river at the ranch. Being there changed those women's lives and they went home and affected other people's lives.

Let's go back to Tootie Bland for a moment. Chris Cox is the only trainer who has won the *Road to the Horse* four times. No one else had done that. He is truly gifted and a great horseman.

Now that the book was off my plate, I switched gears and opened my PowerPoint to work on my speech.

Less than two hours later, I got an email from the editor saying we hit a snag and it would be delayed yet again. Ugh! I screamed some naughty words. It was so bad that I woke up the dogs and they slinked away to the other room to get away from the crazy lady.

Then I remembered my mom saying, "Suck it up, Buttercup. Don't worry, be happy."

Later that day, the horseshoer (or farrier depending on where you live) came to our farm in Minnesota to trim our horses. Being a horseshoer is an art and a science. I appreciate Steve's work for many reasons. First of all, he is very technically proficient. No hoof, no horse. My horses were never lame because of a bad trim job.

For non-horse people, the horse's hooves are like our fingernails, they grow out and need to be trimmed every six weeks. If the horse only walks on nice soft sand or is a mare out in a field with her foal, the horse can go barefoot. But if the horse is used hard or walks on gravel, they need shoes to protect their tender feet. And the angle is also very important. Any woman knows if you wear flats all week and then high heels on Saturday night your back hurts.

NEVER DULL!

I was holding the horses while we chatted. I really like the way Steve treats a horse. He knows that the horse is a prey animal and does not feel safe when the foot is taken away and the horse can't run away. Steve touches the horse on the shoulder and runs his hand down the leg and waits for the horse to give the foot to him rather than abruptly grab the ankle and take the foot away from the horse. Steve asked me, "So what are you up to."

I told him about the delay for my book and kidded him, "I need to get back inside and work my speech for a Christian retreat but I am out here holding a horse for you!"

Steve said, "Oh poor baby! You have big problems don't you? What is your speech about?"

I said, "You're right, it's all about perspective and how you look at it. I have nothing to complain about. Anyway, the theme of the retreat is *Finding Your Purpose.* My speech is about how you will never know how your actions affect others, but God knows. He sees the big picture. God is pulling strings and connecting the dots." I said, "I was so stressed, that I typed TriANGEL C on my slides instead of Triangle C. Because it looked odd, I had to slow down and really look at it. I thought, tri-because God is three in one, Angels and C stands for Christ."

He said, "Ya, that's cool. Where is that ranch?"

"It is in Wyoming. It belongs to Chris Cox."

He said, "Chris Cox is a GREAT guy. I met him this year. He lives in Texas, right?" The horseshoer finished the hoof he was working on and set it down gently. He gave the horse a pat and moved to the other side.

"He does, but he summers in Wyoming." I thought, *wow, what are the odds that these two would overlap? We live in Minnesota. How did Steve meet Chris?*

Steve took a swig of water, stretched his back and picked up the next hoof, "He came to the International Farriers Summit in Ohio in January. He was the keynote speaker at the big banquet and said a horse never needs to be sedated or restrained. He said the horse has been trained incorrectly, it is an owner problem not a horse problem. Everyone there was hanging on his every word. Chris learned that the proceeds from the auction benefitted the *Injured Farriers Fund* and *Hammers and Heroes.*"

Steve bent over to pick up the next foot. The horse would not budge. With his metal hoof trimmers, Steve went tap . . Tap . . **TAP** on the horse's hoof. The INSTANT the horse moved, Steve rewarded the horse and quit tapping.

I asked, *"What is Hammers and Heroes?"*

Steve picked up the foot and gave the horse a pat, "It's a nonprofit that provides therapeutic blacksmithing to military veterans and first responders. On the spot, Chris donated two certificates for a weekend for two of private training to learn about how a horse thinks. In less than four minutes it raised $8000."

I said, "Wow! That story is going to be the lead-in for my speech!"

God gave Chris Cox a great talent to understand horses. Chris found his purpose. God blessed Chris, but that was a by-product of God's true intent. It's all a big circle, all the dots are connected. God affected one man, but that one man affected many more people. Chris will never meet the injured farrier that gets to buy his kids soccer shoes or make his mortgage payment. Chris won't know the person with PTSD that was helped by therapeutic blacksmithing. Because of that training that veteran or first responder now has a purpose and a vocation. They will bless others because that is a lost art and there is a shortage of farriers.

God gave Chris a gift because He knew it would be used to benefit others someday.

Chris is a humble guy and would not toot his own horn. Without the delay, I wouldn't have talked to Steve about my "problems" and I would have never known what Chris did and how he blessed others. And because of the delay, I am able to put that story in the book and it is the perfect introduction to my speech.

I will post the whole speech on my website.

You were right Mom, it's all gonna work out. Don't worry, be happy.

THE BIG PICTURE

Back to my conversation with Pat Parelli, we talked about how important setting goals is. I told Pat what my parents said, "Whatever your mind can conceive, you can achieve. Don't just wish and hope; make it happen."

Pat said:

One weekend, I won the Cal Poly Rodeo and the next day we drove up to Clements and I won the Clements Rodeo. Both of them gave belt buckles, but it was back in 1973 when the price of silver went sky high all of a sudden and the buckles went from a nice beautiful size belt buckle to a itty bitty belt buckle.

So I won these two big rodeos, and I won two tiny rodeo belt buckles.

And I was kind of sad. I'd be kinda like, oh, man, just when I finally win belt buckles, they're little bitty things. And then I said to myself, well, someday I'm gonna live in Clements, and I'm gonna have two little kids and that eventually did happen. And both my kids, my daughter is 42 and my son is 40, have those belt buckles.

Pat talked about all the people that influenced his life: World Champion Bronc Rider Johnny Hawkins, great horsemen like Ray Hunt, Tom Dorrance, Dr. Billy Linfoot, Freddie Ferreira, Troy Henry and others, including my dear old Dad.

NEVER DULL!

Pat said:

I believe in the laws of attraction. I have always been attracted to and try to attract people with good core values. For example, your dad was not just a top level veterinarian, he was a champion in life. Same thing with Johnny Hawkins, he wasn't just a World Champion, he was a champion in life.

So, your dad is one of those, I call them one percenters. If you wanna soar like an eagle, don't fly with turkeys. In other words, everybody that your dad introduced me to or Jack Roddy introduced me to they were all top level people, and that's where that circle of eagles flies around the top of the mountain.

That was really special, not only who your dad was but the circle of influence of his friends. It influenced me to wanna only learn from the best and forget the rest.

Your dad had the reputation of being a great large animal vet and really having a lot of compassion for making sure the animals did well and thrived.

And by then, I was already starting to get a reputation for being able to handle horses that didn't behave the way we wanted them to.

Because that's where I kind of got my start with all these thoughts, and we started talking about how horses feel, think, act and play. Your Dad had already recommended that some people send their horses to me.

We had a relationship of mutual respect for each other. We both cared about animals.

So now, let's rewind a few years and hear a story about a horse that was in our family. I knew all the other stories in this book by heart because we told them so often, but I had completely forgotten this until Pat reminded me about it, and I called Brian to get the rest of the story. I was not around in the late 1980s because, as you will find out in a few chapters, I was off doing my own thing and on the outs with my mom.

In 1976, my grandpa John Roddy bred his good mare to the stallion *Son of Sugar,* and she had a foal. They chose the innovative and highly unusual name of *Sonny* for the colt by *Son of Sugar.*

My family was too busy doing other stuff and did not spend much time thinking up creative names for the horses. They named the roan horse, *Roany*. The sorrel horse, *Red*. We had a *Blackie and Brownie*. Over the years, we had more than one *Brownie,* but never at the same time.

They loved Sugar Bars and Driftwood horses. We had three horses named *Sugar* and two named *Drifter.*

Then Dad really stretched his imagination and cleverly named his grey horse, *Blue* and our next horse, *Red*. But the name *Red* was really confusing because we already had a horse by that name and this new horse was really brown. Oh, and let's not forget the highly inventive and unconventional name of *TC,* which was short for *The Colt.*

Never Dull!

I know I shouldn't make fun of the dead, but I can't help it.

I have to tell you one more thing.

Dad bragged that he was fluent in Spanish and could talk to horses just like Dr. Dolittle. In addition to his "El Photo Grande" comment, when a new client would bring their horse to Dad, he would look into the horse's eye and ask. "Como esta frijole caballo?" The owner would have a puzzled look on their face and Dad would explain, "I just asked him, How you bean horse?"

Oh, Dad.

Anyway, despite his boring name, Sonny was a great horse with natural talent. He was a stallion until he was five and had an attitude. He wasn't mean. He was just very impressed with himself and knew that he was gorgeous. He had confidence out the wazoo. That horse had heart. He was something else.

Jack Roddy's family broke Sonny and did it the right way. Sonny was a handful, and they were partners with him rather than trying to show him who was boss. He was a smart horse, it took all their skills to walk the fine line to harness his energy and still keep the fire lit in his belly.

In the old days of the wild west, *breaking a horse* meant the cowboy roped the horse, tied him down, and stood on top of him. Then the cowboy would blindfold the horse, put on a halter and saddle, mount up, rip off the blindfold, and let 'er buck. A broke horse often meant the horse had a broken spirit.

Thank goodness we have come a long way since then.

I got to ride him in the cutting at the National High School Rodeo Finals in 1985. I stayed out of his way to let him dazzle the judges with his talent, and he won third.

THE BIG PICTURE

When I graduated high school, Sonny became a heeling horse for my brother and the two of them really jelled. Brian has the same demeanor as Dad and goes with the flow. He did not get in Sonny's way or tell him what to do. Sonny was a superstar and put Brian in the right place every time.

Brian and Sonny would lay down a smokin' fast run and Brian, who was usually quiet, would whoop and Sonny would shake his head, snort a little, and flip his long flaxen hair out of his eyes. As Brian would coil the rope up, Sonny would put his ears forward and look at all of his adoring fans in the grandstands. Sonny was sure the audience was clapping for him.

You could tell Sonny got mad if Brian missed. In the team roping, the team can use a total of three loops. If Brian missed, Sonny would not give Brian another shot. Sonny would stand there like a statue and flick his tail up and down. This was Sonny's way of flipping Brian off or telling the header that he didn't handle the steer correctly. Thankfully, Brian hardly missed.

Brian also loved his white calf-roping horse named *Casper*. (*Casper* came to us with that name. If we had raised him from a baby, I am sure his name would have been *Whitey* or maybe even something exotic like *Blue number 2*.)

Tragically, Casper got lame and had to be put down. Even the world's greatest veterinarian couldn't help him. Dad felt terrible. Brian was devastated. Mom knew how he felt. Her horse Chongo died unexpectedly, and she was heartbroken.

The year-end High School Finals Rodeo was coming up for my brother and he was without a calf horse. It was 1986,

NEVER DULL!

Sonny was ten years old, in his prime and the two of them got along well. My parents decided, "*Sonny is the perfect size and has explosive speed. He is a genius. He can do anything.*"

So they sent Sonny to a Calf Roping horse trainer. Sonny caught on quickly and would stop on a dime, but he refused to back up. Sonny felt that backing up and holding the rope was beneath him. It wasn't his idea, and it wasn't something he wanted to do. He would not budge.

Sonny and the trainer did not get along. Sonny was an alpha and used to being in charge. Apparently, the trainer had yet to read the book from the great horseman Tom Dorrance. He said, "Don't fight with your horse. Make the wrong thing difficult and the right thing easy."

The trainer was going to make Sonny submit. The trainer tried every mechanical device he could think of to make Sonny back up.

Sonny was flicking his tail up and down and had his ears back. Every muscle in his body was clenched and he stood like a statue. If Sonny could have talked, he would have said, *Nope. Not gonna do it. If you keep pushing me, I'm gonna get really mad and then we will all be sorry.*

The trainer called and wanted permission to use a shock collar. Brian immediately said no and brought Sonny home.

It is only now as I write this, that I realize how unselfish this was. Brian could have said that he wanted to win at all costs. Brian was in the lead for the year and had enough points that all he needed to do was have a clean run at the finals, Brian would end up in first place and win the buckle. He could toss Sonny aside after Sonny had served his purpose.

Brian chose to do the right thing.

I would like to tell you that I would have done the same thing. But I am not sure that I would have had that wisdom at that age. I was pretty selfish. I was the equivalent of Sonny in the human world. Except Sonny was a lot better looking and much more talented.

Sonny came home. Sonny had won and got his way but was now standing in his pen with nothing to do. Sonny was depressed and so was Brian.

My folks were at a loss for what to do. Brian and Sonny got along great when Brian team roped on him. They were in sync. Now Brian had only two weeks to find another calf horse before the Finals. And even if they were able to find a new horse, there would not be enough time for Brian and the horse to become one and trust each other.

Mom and Dad just knew there had to be a solution to this. They thought, *Don't give up. Think outside the box.*

Ding. A lightbulb went off in Dad's head. Pat Parelli.

Pat had moved from Livermore to Clements, and it had been many years since Dad had seen him. Pat was a big deal by then. Pat could have easily tossed the little people aside because he was flying around in private jets and doing demonstrations for Ronald Reagan, Casey Tibbs, and even the Queen of England.

Dad called Pat, and it was as if no time had passed. Pat did Dad a favor, made room for Sonny in his program and said he would personally work with the horse.

Never Dull!

Pat tells the rest of the story:

Your dad and I had some interactions on horses that had some challenges. And then your brother, Brian, had a horse that was really good, but he wouldn't back up after he roped the calf. Brian came to spend a week with me there in Clements. And of course, your dad came up several times and I taught him how to teach the horse to back up by wiggling the lead rope at him and that sort of thing, instead of putting on a mechanical thing, you know, an electric shock collar and all kinds of things. And I just taught him how to back the horse into the stall, just teaching him to back up whenever you looked at him and then we, Brian and I, would practice him cantering around my arena, which I bought from the Camarillo's and Bob Tallman, and step off and then just go down the rope like, pretend like he roped a calf and then step down and shake the rope at him. Anyway, one thing led to another after a week and then, I guess about a week later, he ended up winning the next rodeo he went to.

That week was life-changing for Sonny. Before Sonny went to Pat's, he was close to being irretrievably ruined by a horse trainer that didn't understand how to motivate a horse. The trainer would have broken his spirit, and Sonny would never forget the anger he felt towards a rider.

THE BIG PICTURE

BRIAN ON SONNY 1987

Sonny was part of our family. There would be no question that we would have kept him even if he became damaged goods. Without Brian making the right call and the intervention from Pat Parelli, Sonny would have been miserable.

Not just for being shocked with a dog collar but for the rest of his life. He would have been standing in his pen, angry that he had been bossed around, angry that a new horse had taken his place and he couldn't do what he loved. He would be angry at everything and not understand what happened and why nobody rode him anymore.

Thanks to God that this story has a happy ending.

NEVER DULL!

Brian took Sonny to Cal Poly and made it into the top ten at the College National Rodeo Finals in Bozeman, Montana in 1992.

Sonny was a member of our family until he died at 32 years old. Four generations enjoyed that horse. My grandpa had him until Sonny was 4 and then gave him to Jack, and then Brian and I rode him and finally, Brian's kids.

The same horse, who was a handful with an attitude, was now babysitting the grandkids.

GRANT AND HEATHER ON
SONNY IN 2000

My mom was a pretty good barrel horse trainer, she said, "Just stay out of your horse's way. Let them think."

That is the same thing that Pat Parelli said about Bob Tallman, "He is so great because he stays out of the way." Let the magic happen.

Mom said, "Don't try to control every step your horse makes. Train them right and trust them to do the right thing."

A person that picks, picks, picks or nags, nags, nags is going make their horse numb and the horse won't be responsive. Or a person who tries to bribe their horse with treats or oats will create an unruly horse that walks all over them. A horse like that will take advantage of the very hand that feeds them.

Some people think they are going to show the horse who's boss. They whip or beat the horse and expect compliance and obedience, but what they get is a horse that shuts down because it is fearful, or the rider causes the horse to get defensive and protect himself. Now the horse is ready to fight and horses never forget.

Go back and swap out the word *horse* for the word *child*. You can learn a lot about parenting by training an animal.

What my dad knew and we learned from watching people like Chris Cox and Pat Parelli work with horses is: It's all about trust and respect.

You can't make an 1100-pound horse do what you want any more than you can make a 16-year-old kid do it your way. It has to be their idea.

NEVER DULL!

The horse and the kid need to have confidence that you will not put them at risk. For a horse, it's all about safety. For a kid, it's all about trust and respect.

Theodore Roosevelt said, *"People don't care how much you know until they know how much you care."*

You can't demand respect or trust. You have to earn it. And you have to be consistent because kids or horses are crafty little buggers; they can sense weakness and have an uncanny ability to get what they want. Don't be harsh, but be firm. Don't weaken or take a shortcut.

My mom knew how to train a horse. But I'm old. Back in the stone ages when I was a kid, she didn't know to apply the same principles to raising kids. I was an alpha. I wasn't going to be bribed, I didn't want to be told what to do, and I wasn't going to do anything unless it was my idea.

Just like Sonny, I was a handful and hard to train.

Chapter 9

AN ANSWER TO PRAYER

After my mom passed, her best friend told me, "I have never heard Marian say, 'Oh, that sounds like a bad idea' or 'That will never work."

She was always so positive and encouraging. Mom thought absolutely anything was possible.

Dad was usually very quiet and didn't talk about his work much. But over dinner in 1979, he said, "I read the most interesting article in a veterinary journal. In Japan, they use acupuncture instead of anesthesia during surgery on dogs. The article said how much faster the recovery is for the animal. It was fascinating."

In typical Mom fashion, she said, "You should do it."

Dad looked at her like she lost her marbles.

Mom said, "You're a smart guy. Go over there and learn all about it. You can be the first large animal vet to bring it to the US. You can do anything."

After much correspondence, which included hiring a translator, Dad decided to go to Japan.

NEVER DULL!

This crazy idea would require him to go to Japan for two months to study under a master and the tuition was expensive. Really expensive. It was a big gamble, but Mom was supportive. After all, he had been supportive of her.

Dad was a well-respected veterinarian, and now he was going to Japan to study acupuncture. His clients thought he had fallen off the deep end. They told him, "You have worked hard to have a great reputation. Why ruin it now by turning into a quack? Don't do it!" They were convinced that nutty Marian had finally worn him down. His customers were cowboys. They love facts and have zero tolerance for garbage. They don't believe in anything touchy-feely.

Either it works, or it doesn't, and cowboys won't pay for anything that didn't work.

Mom did have second thoughts about Dad becoming a quack and pursuing acupuncture, but she never told Dad. He received unwavering support from her that going to Japan was a good idea.

Money was tight, and she just told Dad to fly to Japan and take two months off. She was thinking, *What if it doesn't work? What if acupuncture is all in your head?*

I overheard her confiding to her friend on the phone, "What was I thinking? I've done some stupid stuff before, but this is over the top!"

They chatted for a while, and then I heard Mom say, "It's all going to work out. Everything always does!"

What I learned from that was to stand by your man. They were both extremely loyal to each other. Her other friends would call and complain about their husbands. Mom never did.

An Answer to Prayer

MARIAN ON SUGAR

I know that Dad did some things that drove her nuts and vice-versa, but they never whined or complained about the other one.

Mom's horse Sugar was sired by the great racehorse Sugar Bars. He was challenging for her to train because he thought faster than she did and remembered everything. She had to accelerate her already quick mind to keep up with him. He had explosive speed and was extremely athletic. Even with the stumble at the second barrel at Oakdale Rodeo, he still won second place. She decided to sell Sugar because they needed the money so Dad could go to Japan.

Out of the blue, a wealthy wheat farmer from Washington State called her. He had heard about Sugar and wanted to buy the horse for his daughter. He asked how much she'd take.

She hadn't thought about it yet and blurted out, "$12,000."

"I will send you a deposit."

Cha-ching! $12,000 is the equivalent of $72,000 today.

Two months of no income was doable now. Dad was on his way to Japan.

Mom went to Catholic school and believed in God; He just wasn't part of our everyday life. We never went to church on Sundays. We were too busy going to rodeos. That was the priority at the time.

However, many years later, she told me that selling Sugar was an answer to a prayer.

Because she was so busy getting her horse sold, Christmas snuck up on her. On Christmas Eve, she realized she HAD to go shopping. She rode Sugar in the morning, unsaddled him quickly, jumped in her Oldsmobile, and raced to Bullock's department store in Walnut Creek. She didn't have time to change out of her boots and spurs because the store was closing early for Christmas.

As she hustled into the store, Mom saw a woman in a red jacket with her son waiting in line to sit on Santa's lap. The woman looked down her nose at Mom's spurs and sneered.

AN ANSWER TO PRAYER

The woman looked like she was thinking, *You're not going to win Mother of the Year in that outfit.*

Mom went to the second floor and got clothes for us kids. Just what every kid wants from Santa . . . clothes. Mom paid for her purchases and started down the escalator to the first floor with two large shopping bags in each hand. She thought, *Maybe I'll see some See's candies or something festive on the first floor.*

She heard an announcement over the loudspeaker. "The store will be closing in thirty minutes. Don't forget there is free gift wrapping on the second floor. We wish you a Merry Christmas."

She heard that and thought, *Oh, perfect!* Rather than spend time going down the escalator to the first floor, all the way around, and back up the other escalator, she turned around and started to climb back up. She reasoned this was much faster.

After all, she was only three steps into it . . . then four . . . then five. She started to jog and was holding steady. Now she was getting winded. Other shoppers saw her, and a semi-circle began to form at the top. No one wanted to go down the escalator and do battle with a woman who was so clearly on a mission. She must have looked dangerous.

The woman in red and her son were waiting at the top for the now winded Mom to get out of the way. The woman grabbed her son's hand and pulled him back, like a mama bear protecting her cub from harm.

Mom reached the top and lunged forward like a racer crossing the finish line at the Boston Marathon. At the very last stair, her spur caught, and she tripped. The weight of her shopping bags propelled her forward, and she skidded across the tile floor. Her belt buckle made a screeching noise, and her bags went everywhere. There she was, sprawled out in front of the crowd. The crowd was too shocked at the spectacle to move, and no one came forward to help her.

At first, she pretended like nothing happened but realized she couldn't stand up because she had banged her knee. She started laughing and crawled on all fours to her shopping bags. She stood up, regained composure, and tried to conceal her limp as she gracefully walked toward the gift wrapping station.

The woman in red snatched her son's hand and harshly said, "See, I told you never to play on the escalator. This is what happens. You look like a fool."

Mom stuck her tongue out at the lady and smiled at the kid.

Sadly, this would not be Mom's last difficulty with multiple floors at a shopping center.

The fact that cowboys were so doubtful of acupuncture turned out to be a good test. Horses cannot understand a placebo. You can't tell them they are going to feel better.

Jack Roddy always took excellent care of his horses. His horse Roany was fed well but wasn't running as hard as he used to, and Jack could tell something was off, but he couldn't put his finger on it.

JACK ON ROANY, JIMMY ON THE
LEFT ON BILLY RED

The horse had been steadily declining and did not have the spark he used to. Supplements and blood tests were getting too expensive.

Jack did not need a lawn ornament. He reasoned it was just age and sold the horse cheaply to Mom. He knew Roany would have a good life with his brother-in-law, the veterinarian, and Roany would become a nice kid's horse for my brother and me. The horse previously described as electric was now dull and sluggish.

Never Dull!

Mom had a welcome back party for Dad when he returned from Japan. Among other people, both of her brothers came. Dad couldn't wait to show off his new skills to Jack and Jimmy, even though he knew they were a tough crowd. They were highly skeptical and would call a spade a spade, no matter who you were.

Dad said Roany would be his first victim. Mom held the horse's halter, and Jack and Jimmy crowded around to get a closer look while Dad put the acupuncture needles in.

Dad said, "This horse's coat is dull because his hair is standing up. When I treat him, his hair will lie down. He will shake his head and roll his eyes. Then he will lick his lips because the energy has been blocked. When the naturally occurring electricity in his body can make a complete loop, it will stimulate the pituitary and salivary glands."

Nothing happened. The horse just stood there. Dad frowned. "Sometimes it takes a little while." Dad rechecked his needles. "Sometimes it takes several treatments."

Jimmy said, "How long will this take? This horse might roll his eyes back in his head because he is dead! Come on, Nolan!"

Jack said to Jimmy, "Our sister has married a duck! He's a quack."

Dad laughed. He was used to being teased and didn't let them bother him. Mom chewed her lip but didn't say a peep.

Several minutes went by before they saw a change. Roany did look better.

Jimmy said, "Maybe it's because we've been standing here so long that the sun finally came out." He looked up to see if the sky had changed. Nope. He moved to the other side to get a better view, "Jack! Look at this. He is glistening. His hair is shiny!"

Roany shook his head. He rolled his eyes and licked his lips. He blinked as if he had just woken up and yawned several times. His eyes got brighter, and he started looking around for some food.

Jack teased, "Marian! I want my horse back!"

"Nope, a deal's a deal," she said smugly.

Dad smiled proudly, "See! You all doubted me."

Roany curled his head around and nudged Dad's belly with his nose. If the horse could have talked, he would have said, "Thanks, Dude."

Jack said, "If I had not been standing here, I would not have believed it. My buddies will say you gave him a shot full of vitamins or somethin' when I wasn't looking. Nope. This is the real deal."

Mom started barrel racing on Roany and wound up winning several rodeos on him. Once again, Jack Roddy got no mount money for his horse.

NEVER DULL!

MARIAN ON ROANY

An Answer to Prayer

In 1984, Dad studied equine chiropractic with Graham Boyd from Australia.

Rose Webb had qualified for the National Finals Rodeo in barrel racing in 1986. She made an appointment with Dad because her horse, Dandy, didn't just feel right. She said he wasn't turning to the left like he used to.

I missed school so I could be Dad's assistant. Mom was there too because she was friends with Rose and Mom knew how Dad could focus on an animal and become grouchy and rude. She was there to help Dad improve his bedside manner. Dad was not going to win any awards for Mr. Congeniality.

Rose spent every waking moment with Dandy. She knew every nuance of this horse and told Dad in great detail what his symptoms were. Dad asked Rose, "When he rolls, does he go all the way over?"

"Oh." Rose shook her head, "He doesn't like to roll. He doesn't like to get dirty."

Dad snorted and rolled his eyes. Mom gave him a sharp look. When Rose wasn't looking, she mouthed to him, "Lighten up."

Dad palpated the horse from head to tail and pressed hard on his muscles.

Rose said, "Should I be massaging him like that?"

"No, Not like I'm doing. Don't press as hard as I am right now. I'm trying to see if he flinches. That means his neck or his back is out of alignment. You could massage the muscles, though." He stopped pressing hard on Dandy and smiled at Rose. "Ice is an excellent treatment to reduce inflammation. Fill a Styrofoam cup with water and put it in the freezer. When

141

it's frozen, rip about an inch of Styrofoam off. Turn it over and treat the sore muscles. That way, your hand won't get cold."

Mom smiled and nodded like a proud mother at a spelling bee.

He went back to pressing where he had left off. "So you say he doesn't like to roll anymore. Did he used to?" Dad pressed on Dandy's hip. Dandy's butt dropped toward the ground so fast that Dad's hands stayed in the air.

Dad smiled widely. "I think we have our answer." He patted Dandy's neck and said. "Take him into the arena over there. I am going to get some tranquilizer."

Dad came back with a syringe, "Dandy is a smart horse. He knows I intend to give him a shot. Rose, you hold his head with the halter." He uncapped the needle and held it near Dandy's jugular vein. "When I nod, you move his head towards me about four inches." He nodded. Dandy didn't even flinch when the needle pierced his skin.

Dad said, "It's similar to when your dentist gives you a shot and wiggles your cheek. Your brain concentrates on the movement and doesn't feel the needle."

Rose said, "Huh. Interesting"

"This tranquilizer will take ten minutes to take effect. Dandy's not going to be knocked out. He can still stand, but he won't resist me. He severely outweighs me, and I need every advantage. It's good you came to a real vet because some other guys who do this don't have veterinary licenses. They cannot use tranquilizers or take X-rays. Sometimes your horse is off because of a medical problem, which only a vet could diagnose."

She nodded.

"His sacroiliac is out. That is this joint on us." He turned his back and put his hand below his belt and above his tailbone. "Okay, Dandy is relaxed now. Heather, you stand on the other side of his hip and push it against me." He picked up the horse's back leg, so it was folded up like a flamingo standing on one leg.

He quickly pulled the leg toward the sky and POP. I could feel it in my hands, and we all heard it. "That noise was the gas that is inside the joint. They call it a dry joint. It was frozen up." He dusted off his hands and moved to adjust Dandy's neck.

After a little while, Dandy woke up fully from the tranquilizer. Dad told Rose to turn him loose in the arena so he could roll.

She said proudly, "I told you. He doesn't like to get dirty. He won't roll. He is a prima donna and waits for me to brush him."

Dad snapped at her, "That's BS. Every horse likes to roll."

Mom whispered to me, "She didn't come here to be reprimanded."

Dandy walked around, he sniffed, and pawed the ground. He started to lie down and then bounced back up.

Dad said, "It takes a horse ten days to forget the pain. Even though the pain is no longer there, the horse will protect itself." Dad clucked to Dandy and clapped his hands a few times. Dandy trotted a few steps, stopped, and bent his head down to scratch his ankle with his nose. A truck drove by on the main road; the driver honked his horn and waved to Dad.

NEVER DULL!

This spooked Dandy. He jerked his head up, squealed, and bolted. Then he stopped abruptly and snorted like a dragon. Rose said, "He feels good. He's sassy." Dandy ran back to the same spot where he pawed, sniffed again, and flopped down and rolled like a pig.

He grunted and moaned. He scratched the middle of his back with his feet in the air. His nose quivered when he put his front legs out in front so he could scratch his belly. He rolled over to one side and rubbed his neck like a maniac.

Rose was crying. Mom was crying. I was crying. Everyone was crying. Even Dad was a little misty.

Dad cleared his throat, "Told ya. Every horse likes to roll."

Chapter 10

THE ISLAND OF MISFIT TOYS

Many of Dad's clients either couldn't or didn't want to pay their vet bills—especially ranchers. Cattle are a business, not a pet. Dad had a soft heart and would try anything.

A tractor ran over a calf, and his front left leg was mangled. The rancher brought him to Dad's clinic to see if anything could be done. Dad said, "No, we will have to amputate."

"I'll just shoot him then." The rancher said.

"No, no. Let me see what I can do."

"I am not paying for it."

"I'll do it for free."

"All right, he's yours. I'm giving him to you."

So Dad amputated the calf's leg and called him Howard. I am not sure where the name Howard came from. He said if it were a heifer, he would have called her Eileen.

Ha, ha. Good one, Dad.

He built a prosthetic leg for Howard and strapped it on with a worn-out horse cinch from the tack room. (Side note, a cinch that my mom had not yet thrown away during spring cleaning.)

NEVER DULL!

The fake leg worked great, except that Howard grew rapidly, and Dad kept having to make a new, larger leg. When the leg would fall off, Howard would bellow and wail until Dad or one of us kids would go out there and strap his leg on for him again.

Another client had a steer that looked pregnant. Dad went to the ranch to look at the steer. Thankfully, he was a real cattleman and had a chute. The rancher said, "He looks like a hot air balloon."

Dad nodded, "Yep, it's a water belly." He went to his vet rig to get a stainless steel straw that was sharp on one end. Picture a giant hypodermic needle, and you get the idea.

Dad knew precisely where to slap that needle under the steer's belly, and urine came out with great force. The stomach deflated, and Dad said, "This poor guy has rocks in his pee-pee. He can't go to the bathroom."

The rancher said, "I'll load him up then and take him to the butcher. My wife said the freezer is getting empty."

"I'm not sure that's a good idea. That meat may not taste good depending on how long it's been since he peed."

The rancher frowned.

Dad said, "I have an idea. I'll give him a roto-rooter or re-plumb the whole system."

The rancher only saw dollar signs and shook his head. "I've heard about your Frankenstein experiments. I don't want any part of it! I'll drop him off at your place, Doc. You can have that steer."

The guy backed his trailer up to the operating room. I got to be Dad's assistant. Dad gave the steer a tranquilizer and opened the gate for the steer to go in. That steer walked around like a drunk and passed out almost perfectly on the operating table. Dad repositioned the steer and signaled me to raise the hydraulic lift.

Dad decided the roto-rooter would be too short-lived. He said, "I want to try something else." I held the suture kit while Dad cut free the steer's urethra and routed it under the skin, through the legs, and out the back.

Dad declared it the world's first sex-change operation on a bovine. The re-route worked great. Unfortunately, Dad made the hole too small, and the pee shot straight out ten feet.

A few months later, we got another calf. Dad got an emergency phone call in the middle of the night to do a cesarian on a cow. He told the rancher, "Bring the cow to the clinic, and I'll meet you there."

I was 12 years old, and Dad woke me up to see if I wanted to help. Of course, I did. I loved to help my dad, but I also knew this meant no school the next day.

The cow looked terrible when the rancher unloaded her into the operating room. Dad asked, "How long has she been in labor?"

"Three days."

Dad sighed. "Why didn't you call me on day one?"

"Because I thought she would be able to calve on her own. And your vet bill is too expensive. Now I want to see if you can save her."

Dad rolled his eyes and quickly started the surgery. He opened up her belly, got the calf out of her uterus, and set it on the ground. The calf looked like a rag doll. Dad wordlessly looked at me, sighed, and shook his head.

Dad was sewing up the cow when the rancher saw her take her last breath. The rancher turned on his heel, got in his truck, and left.

Dad rolled his eyes, "Well, I'll send him a bill, but I know he won't pay. I'll finish stitching her up so her guts don't fall all over the place." Our black lab, Molly, was Dad's shadow. She was never more than three feet from him. She went to the calf and started licking his wet head. The calf flinched.

I screamed, "Dad! Look!"

"How about that! Pick him up by the back legs and sling him around. His lungs are full of amniotic fluid. You got to get it out. Then set him down and let the dog keep licking him. That is what a mother cow would do. The licking stimulates his nervous system."

"He's not breathing, Dad."

Dad was still sewing the cow up. "Put your hands under his ribs and inflate his lungs. Pick him up again and sling him around."

I did. I shook my head and said, "No luck, he's dead."

"Don't give up. Give him mouth to mouth."

"Seriously?"

"Heather, do what I say!"

He nodded. I held the little calf's mouth closed and blew as hard as I could. Then I would pull and push on his rib cage. He started to come to life. Dad told me I could have the calf.

The calf, the dog, and I slept in a stall under a heat lamp that night. The dog was deeply conflicted the next day and couldn't decide if she wanted to follow Dad around or stay with the calf.

She stayed with the calf.

I called him Mickey and bottle-fed him. The dog loved feeding time because she would lick the milk that ran down Mickey's cheeks. Mickey was confused about who his mom was. He thought it might be the dog because she was the one that licked him, but I was the one that gave him the milk. He couldn't decide whom he loved more. Just like the dog, he was also deeply conflicted about who he loved best.

MICKEY

While I was at school during the day, Mickey followed the dog around everywhere. And the dog followed my dad around everywhere. Both animals slept underneath the desk in the clinic. This was fine until Mickey started to grow. One day, he stood up, and the whole desk went with him. Dad said Mickey was no longer allowed inside the clinic.

Poor Mickey had to stay outside with the other misfit toys.

When Mickey was a baby, I taught him how to butt people. Especially my little brother and his friends. When they were playing football and had their butts up for the hike, I would point at the boy's fanny, and Mickey would come running and smack their rear ends. This was cute when he was a baby. But when Mickey grew to 800 pounds, he became a menace.

A few months later, Dad got a phone call from the Veterinary Clinic at UC Davis. They heard about all the innovative things he was doing and wanted to come for a tour. The operating table, the acupuncture and chiropractic, the

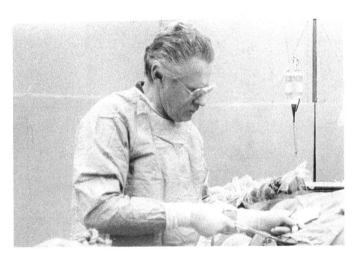

NOLAN DOING SURGERY ON THE
OPERATING TABLE

prosthetic limbs, and the peritoneal urethrostomy. Also known as the high heifer procedure. UC Davis had taught that, but steers never lived long enough to see if the surgery was a success. Our steer was a pet and soon-to-be a celebrity.

Oh boy! This was so exciting. We had to make sure Howard's leg fit and get everything else ready. We cleaned and swept for a week. The clinic looked like a showplace.

A group of six senior professors arrived, and Dad showed them the operating room. They were impressed.

He showed them acupuncture on a client's horse. They were very impressed.

Dad was getting cocky, and it was then that things started to fall apart.

He told me to catch one of our horses, and he would demonstrate chiropractic. I brought the horse into a stall that had rubber mats. While I was waiting for Dad, the horse urinated. *Dang it!* I didn't want a puddle of pee under the horse, so I rushed out and grabbed a scoop of wood shavings to soak up the pee.

Dad came in and told them, "Now, I will demonstrate how to adjust the horse's hip."

Dad was six-foot-three and a strong guy. He gave the leg a heave-ho, and the horse's standing leg slipped on the wet mat, and down the horse went with a thud.

He was a kid's horse and used to crazy behavior. He thought it was part of the training program and lay there like a stone. Dad was embarrassed. He told the group. "Would you believe me if I said I did that on purpose?"

The group of vets laughed nervously. I jiggled the lead rope and the horse bounced back up.

Never Dull!

Dad ushered the group away from the horse barn. "Uh, let's go see the cattle now."

We all walked over to the cattle pen. Dad opened the gate, and the group filed in. The professors had been in a classroom most of their lives and stepped carefully to avoid the poop. The three steers were at the far end of the pen. Dad said, "Heather, go get some grain so the cattle will come over here."

I ran and got a bucket of grain. While Dad was talking to the group, his back faced the cattle. I came running while shaking the bucket, "Come on, boys! Howard! Mickey! He-She!" Dad jerked his head and glared at me.

"Sorry," I was supposed to know we did not use that word in public.

When the cattle heard the grain in the bucket, they started stampeding toward us. Mickey and He-She were bucking and making a beeline toward us. Poor Howard. He tried to run, but his leg fell off. He stood there on three legs and cried and cried. It was such a pitiful sight.

When Mickey got close, all 1,300 pounds butted my dad and knocked him off his feet. The He-She was the first one to the bucket and was peeing all over everyone.

Dad got up from the ground and laughed. "I'm so sorry. This was not how I pictured it in my head."

They told him not to worry. This was a day they would never forget.

Chapter 11

Laugh at Yourself

Before I tell this next story, I should come clean and reveal something I am embarrassed to share. As my friend says, It's time for me to open my kimono and share everything.

When I laugh, I pee my pants. My mom does too!

In our defense, this is hereditary. My grandmother had it. Mom had it. I have it. Thankfully I have two sons, but if I ever have granddaughters, they will likely have it too.

Let's go back in time to 1981 when I was 15. I was a tomboy, and the only thing I cared about was riding horses. I was not into clothes or makeup or anything girly.

Mom was always dressed to the nines in the latest fashions. Her friend Leslie dresses very conservatively but is also hysterically funny. They were a good balance for each other. Mom was like a brightly colored bird flitting to and fro, and Leslie was her rock.

Mom could talk anyone into anything and convinced Leslie to become her business partner. They opened a women's clothing boutique called *Something to Crow About* at the

Never Dull!

Danville Hotel. Mom and Leslie were going to San Francisco to the wholesale clothing mart for a buying trip. I was invited to go along with them. Mom hoped this would cause me to appreciate the importance of fashion.

It was early in the morning, and my mom grabbed her coffee and yelled at me, "Heather, get up. It's time to go." I would be on time for horse events but not shopping events.

While she waited for me, she started her white Cadillac and ran the AC full blast, so her makeup would not melt.

I popped on yesterday's clothes, grabbed breakfast, and jumped in the car. I wore white Nike tennis shoes with a red swoosh, very tight Wrangler jeans, and a Cal Poly sweatshirt with a grease stain on the front. I should add that Mom refused to buy me larger jeans because I was chubby and needed to lose weight. The rationale was that smaller jeans would motivate me to push myself back from the table. Or, as she lovingly called it, the trough.

Mom saw my outfit. "Heather! You can't be seen like that. You have tons of clothes that I bought you. Go put something more appropriate on. And put that muffin back!"

On the way back in the house, I inhaled the muffin and grabbed another one to scarf down while I got dressed. I ran back and jumped in the car.

When she saw me, she blanched. "Did you do this on purpose?"

"No! I think this looks good." I was sincere. I choose my favorites. I wore a red satin jacket, black stirrup pants, purple leg warmers, and sandals. The jacket was too small and only went halfway down my arms. But I have to say; the leg warmers completed the outfit. They were all the rage in the 1980s. I was proud of myself.

She rolled her eyes. "Put the sweatshirt back on, maybe people will think you're homeless and I am adopting you."

"MOM!"

"Oh, Heather. I'm only kidding. You're too serious. Lighten up."

I ran back into the house and got a clean sweatshirt. I hopped back in, she put the Caddy in drive, and we sped off to pick up Leslie. She winked at me. "It will all be OK."

"Thanks, Mom."

"I'll just tell people you're Leslie's kid."

"MOM!"

After marathon shopping, Mom suggested Irish coffees at The Buena Vista Bar. I had my driving permit, meaning they had a designated driver. Leslie said, "Why not! Sounds like fun!"

The shopping center at Ghirardelli Square is near The Buena Vista. At that time, it had four levels. Parking on the underground level, two floors of shops, and a five-star restaurant on the entire top floor.

This little piece of information is important to know; the elevator opened directly to the restaurant, with floor-to-ceiling windows and a dramatic view of the San Francisco Bay. When the elevator doors opened, the maître d' was waiting with a white linen napkin draped over his arm. He bowed and, just

NEVER DULL!

like Vanna White, swung his free arm to show the amazing view of the Golden Gate Bridge and Alcatraz Island.

After Mom and Leslie tossed back a few Irish coffees, we were ready to go home and walked two blocks back to Ghirardelli Square. It took us a while to find the elevator to go down one level to our car. Construction was going on, and we were unaware that the elevator buttons were wired incorrectly.

Whenever I pressed P for Parking, the elevator would go to a random level. It would go up to 2, down to 1, and then up to the restaurant. The doors opened, and maître d', with a napkin over his arm, bowed and welcomed us in.

"Oh dear!" I pushed the button again.

Mom was frustrated with me, "Heather, stop screwing around!" She pushed me out of the way and took control of the buttons. She pressed P. The elevator went to 2, and we started to giggle. She mashed P again. The elevator stopped at 1, and a nicely dressed couple got on and pushed the button for the restaurant.

I distinctly remember what the woman wore. She had on beige suede shoes, a matching suede shirt, and a scarlet silk top. Mom told the couple how nice they looked and then nodded at me.

I must have made a face because Mom started laughing. The couple looked at each other uncomfortably. Mom crossed her legs and covered her mouth, a telltale sign that something bad was about to happen. Leslie tried her best to be stern. "Don't do it, Marian! Don't do it!"

The couple moved closer to the doors to distance themselves from my mom. The doors opened, and the couple stepped off. Because Mom was doubled over and now useless, Leslie stepped in, pounded the button, and screamed at it. "P! P! P!" The doors closed, but the elevator didn't move. Now we were all laughing uncontrollably.

My mom crumpled to the floor. Leslie pleaded, "Oh, Marian, no! Please don't!" A yellow puddle started to form. Leslie said flatly, "At least you didn't ruin her suede shoes."

That's all it took. I fell to the floor and peed my pants too. Leslie shrieked, "Aggghhh. A duet!" And like a gymnast, she used the handrails to get her feet off the floor and pushed the button again with her heel.

The doors opened again at the restaurant. Leslie grabbed the napkin from the maître d' and threw it into the puddle, "Don't mind us! Ta-ta!"

Finally, we got down to Floor 1 and found a bathroom. We took our underwear off and washed them out in the sink. We attempted to dry our pants, but the bathroom was out of hand towels, and we had to use the forced-air dryer. All of this while Leslie gave a running commentary about how absurd this situation was. Mom warned Leslie, "Don't say anything funny, or I'll pee my pants again."

The main door to the restroom opened, and a woman started to walk in. Leslie grabbed the door and shooed her away. "There's a hazardous waste spill in here. You can't come in." The woman looked puzzled. Leslie snapped at her, "Beat it!"

I drove home across the Bay Bridge with Leslie's head stuck out the window like a dog because she said she needed fresh air because of our soiled bloomers. Mom was in the back seat crying with laughter. Thankfully, our bladders were empty, and there was no danger of us peeing in the car.

Shortly before that, another tragic incident occurred.

I was not very athletic, and I had terrible posture. I could ride a horse, but that's about it. I could barrel race and rope, but I was a total disaster at goat tying. I would try to dismount and fall flat on my face every time.

For graduation from Junior High, Mom bought me a darling pink dress and styled my hair. After watching me stomp across the stage in three strides, she knew something must be done. In an attempt to make me more graceful, she enrolled all six feet of me in gymnastics. There were six of us in the class, five petite girls who averaged 90 pounds each, and then there was Heather, six feet and 180 pounds. It did not go well.

Then she enrolled me in a modeling class. The idea was that it would make me poised, refined, and well-mannered. Everyone there aspired to be a beauty queen except me. I was there against my will. I did it to make my mom happy.

Actually, that's not true. I really did want to be more coordinated. I should have applied myself more in that class. Years later, when I joined the military and graduated from officer's school, the entire class was supposed to march in formation so the Commandant could review the troops.

They gave me a flag and said, "Stand here on this X. Do not march, or you will ruin everything."

The graduation ceremony was the culmination of six weeks at AMS-the Academy of Military Science, or as my son calls it - the Academy Minimum Standards. He went to the Air Force

Academy for four years. He said it was a free $400,000 education shoved up your fanny one nickel at a time.

I'm like my mom. I do everything fast. It only took me six weeks to become an Officer, and it took him four years! For those of you familiar with the rivalry between the Air National Guard and the quote, *real* Air Force, you will get this joke. I went off on a tangent; so sorry; back to the story.

Finally, Mom gave up on modeling school. It just wasn't going to happen.

My dad was not so easily deterred. He was an athlete in his youth and would not accept defeat. He just knew I had it in me.

One day, the whole family went to the Crow Canyon Racquetball Club. Dad and Brian were playing against me and Mom. This was supposed to be a fun family outing.

Dad was starting to get mad at me because I was screwing around. He barked, "Straighten up and try harder." More proof that he did not have a very good bedside manner. When he was focused on something, he was not very congenial.

Mom wasn't into playing racquetball. She would rather be riding her horse. She mouthed at me, "He's getting mad."

I giggled.

She whispered covertly, "Heather! Be serious, or his head is going to explode, and then I am going to make you clean this up. Because it is all your fault."

I giggled, "But you are the one making it worse."

Dad looked at Mom sharply. She soberly said, "I am so sorry. I should have realized what we have here. We are messing up our chance to go pro. A recruiter is probably out there right now looking for someone with our natural talent. You're right. We need to stop screwing around. There will be no more fun. Heather! Stop laughing."

When Dad would turn his back, she would impersonate him, and I would laugh.

Dad spun around and glared at her. She stood at attention and saluted him. "Sorry, Sir, no excuse, Sir."

Now Dad was mad at both of us. He served and whacked the ball with such incredible force that it hit the far wall, sailed over our heads, hit the back wall, bounced off that wall and hit me in the back of the head, hit the back wall again, and then bounced between my legs.

That's all it took. I collapsed to the floor and peed my pants. A puddle started to form on the hardwood floor.

Mom said, "Oh, I know how you feel. I'll go get a towel."

Dad was so mad. He was beyond reason. "Do not help her. She will clean this up! It's the only way she will learn."

I was trying so hard not to laugh. I rolled over and crawled like a baby out of my puddle. I got up and wiped my wet hands on my pants. Mom and I went to the locker room to get a towel. We were dying laughing.

When we returned to the court, we straightened up. Mom pointed to the puddle and ordered me, "Cinderella, clean this mess up."

Finally, Dad realized how completely ridiculous this was and we all started to laugh.

Chapter 12

THE BARTER SYSTEM

Dad felt he was born a few years too late. He cherished the old ways of doing things. If Mom was the queen of multi-tasking, he was the undisputed king of bartering. As you will see, he would trade anybody for anything.

My son, Ryan, told the following story at his Celebration of Life in 2018.

Ryan

In defense of Nolan, my mom painted him in a bad picture, saying he demonized this little girl and made this little Barbie cuss in front of her grandparents. She harbors a little grudge because back when she was a kid, she had really bad teeth. All of us do because of her. (laughter)

So Nolan says to his client, Hey, my little girl needs some braces. And he says, "Well, I have some horses that need to be looked at. I'll give her braces if you look at my horses." So he slaps some braces on her. He gets those teeth nice and straight.

NEVER DULL!

But what do you know? The week that those braces need to come off, his horse needs to be looked at again. So he says to Nolan, "Sorry to say, but your daughter has some teeth problems. We're going to have to put some more braces on." And so bam, he threw some more braces on, and then what do you know? Those are about to come off, and he's got another horse that needs to be looked at. And this continued for several years until finally, it was prom night, I think, and she had headgear on! (laughter)

Finally, the orthodontist's horse died. Thank goodness. Otherwise, I would have had to wear braces to my wedding.

One of my favorite stories about Dad and his love of the barter system involved a horse. Dad had a client who couldn't pay her vet bill for surgery on her good mare. Dad traded her the surgery for her two-year-old halter-broke gelding. She said, "He is gentle as a lamb. He's a sweet horse and very friendly but maybe a little bit skittish."

Dad was very unselfish. Brian and I got all the good broke horses. Dad wanted to turn this horse into a roping horse for himself and asked his friend Steve Cosca to get the horse broke. Steve was a good hand and made his living at cowboying and breaking horses.

STEVE COSCA ON "HEAVEN SENT"
AT THE COW PALACE -1973 FOXIE
PHOTO

The following is a transcription of Steve's Story:

I rodeoed professionally for 15 years. I went to the national finals twice in the Bareback Riding in '72 and '73. I also rode bulls. And after '75, I stayed closer to home. And I still rode it every weekend. That's really how I made my living.

Your Dad and I had this horse together, a partnership deal. And the way we got it was your dad had a customer that couldn't afford to pay her bill, but she had this two-year-old horse, and she offered to give the horse to Nolan. So when Nolan received the horse, he called me and asked me if I would start the colt for him. And I said, "Sure, I'll ride him for you. I offered to do the training, and we would partner on the colt." So as it went on, the horse did like to buck. He bucked pretty good, too. He bucked me off, matter of fact, once or twice. But he was a nice horse. He was gentle. You could walk up to him, and he was good to be around. The only thing he did, he did like to hump up and buck a little bit.

One afternoon, I was in a big hurry, had to go somewhere, and I run down to the barn to feed the two horses down there, and he was one of them. And he happened to be in the box stall. And the way our gate was set up, it was only like a two-bar gate. So I just ducked through the gate to go to feed him, well I spooked him. He didn't realize I was coming in and he kicked me and broke my jaw. Well, it was a stupid deal on my end of it. I should have taken my time and made sure he knew where I was. But anyhow, that's how he got his name because he broke my jaw and from then on, we called him Jaw Breaker. I needed to heal up and I sent him back to Nolan. He said, "Should I start riding him?"

I said, "No! He's rank."

The Barter System

While Steve healed up, he sent the horse back to my dad. Mom was getting irritated that Jaws was taking up too much space. She said this horse was too ugly to be in our string. Her brother Jimmy was friends with the Hartnell Rodeo Coach, John Larrick.

JAW BREAKER AS A TWO YEAR OLD

Jimmy Roddy tells the rest of the story.

So Marian was mad. She said, "We are not going to have this ugly horse on our place. I'm not going to feed him. He's gotta go. He's going to make a bucking horse." She called me and I said, "Well sure, you can try him at Hartnell." I called John Larrick.

And so she drove down. We unload the horse and he's nuzzling John and I. He's a nice little horse. And then she drove off and Larrick looked at me, "He ain't gonna make it."

Never Dull!

So we led him down to the chutes, the bronc riders were ready and he was nice in the chute. They saddled him up no problem. He's standing there, quiet and nice as can be. So the Bronc rider nodded his head and, WHOA! Look out! Katy bar the door. The horse bucked like you couldn't believe.

Larrick didn't want to overdo it, so he only bucked him maybe four or five times. And then he got him in the draw at Salinas. And who draws him but Chucky Morris? And Chuck is not happy. He was mad because here is a horse that has never been bucked at a PRCA rodeo.

Chucky gets on him, nods his head and wins first. The picture was famous, they used it for a poster, on bottles of wine, everything.

So they sell him to John Growney that day. Growney took him up to Red Bluff and turned him out with his bucking horses. And when you go by the Growney Ranch on Highway 5, you see that one little cliff close to the highway. Well all the horses were circling there and Jaws was on the outside and he must have got pushed off. Two days later there was no more Jaws. He was gone."

CHUCK MORRIS RIDING JAWBREAKER AT SALINAS
RODEO -1983

Chapter 13

RANCHEROS VISITADORES

Every year in May, my dad would go on the RV ride or Rancheros Visitadores, which is Spanish for "Visiting Ranchers." It was the brainchild of a small group of prominent Santa Barbarans who wished to commemorate the important role horsemanship and ranching had played in the history of California.

In the late 1800s, ranchers would drive their cattle to nearby Missions, and there they would meet up with other ranchers and drive to the following Mission until all the cattle were brought to market.

Every year since 1930, the RV Ride, as it's commonly known, is ten days of riding, roping, singing, and playing pranks on each other. To be invited, you have to be a good sport. Eight hundred businessmen and cowboys, separated into twenty camps, have a blast for ten days. Think of it as a summer camp for grown men meets frat party, and you get the idea.

On the first day of the ride, the RV members parade through downtown Solvang on horseback and assemble on the lawn of the Santa Ynez Mission to receive a blessing from the priest followed by a 25-mile trail ride to camp. Dad was always very popular because he would go around and give each horse a cocktail before everyone would ride their horses in the parade. The cocktail was a small dose of tranquilizer to take the edge off horses that only got ridden a few times a year. He always drove his vet rig down to the RV ride to be ready to stitch up a horse or sometimes a cowboy. Whatever was needed, Dad was your man.

His friend Gene St. John, Jr. told me this story.

When I would see him some mornings on the ride, he would look at me and ask, "How you feel'n?" He asked because I probably looked like death warmed over.

He told me, "Get a cup of orange juice and come to my vet rig."

I would always do what I was told. I followed him to his truck and he extracted some liquid out of a vial with a syringe and a needle. I thought to myself, there is no way he is going to stick that thing in me! Then he squirted a dose of horse painkillers in my orange juice and sent me on my way. God bless Nolan Sharp!

NOLAN AND JACK RODDY

Jack Roddy sponsored Dad in 1974. They were in the same camp, and team roped together often.

Dad was quiet and operated below the radar. He was the opposite of the type A family he married into. Everyone trusted him, and he was the last guy you would suspect to do anything naughty.

In his vet rig, Dad had a bag of IV fluids with a long plastic tube. He asked Jack Roddy to help tape the bag between his shoulder blades and secure it with Vet Wrap. He ran the plastic tube down and around so it came out of his underwear. He told Jack to follow him to where the Chili Cook-Off was being held.

NEVER DULL!

Everyone there was ultra-competitive. To win first in anything was a big deal. It did not matter if it was team roping, Chili Cook-Off, or pig scramble.

When Dad approached the winning chili, he unzipped his pants and said, "Here is what I think of your 'effin chili." Jack pressed on the IV, and Dad appeared to pee in Buck McCullough's chili.

NOLAN "PEEING" IN THE CHILI

Rancheros Visitadores

The other guy devised a plan of how to get Jack and Dad back. Everyone knows that Jack Roddy has a sweet tooth. One camp invited Jack over for a drink and had some brownies on the table. A guy named Frank Morehardt secretly put some Ex-Lax in those brownies. Thank goodness it was not pot; some of the RV members have top-secret clearances and need to go back and pass a random drug test.

The bartender giggled while Jack ate one brownie after another. The Ex-Lax took effect in a little while, and Jack spent the entire night in the latrine.

Pigs were brought in for a pig scramble the next day. That night, Jack roped the pigs, and Dad tranquilized them. They broke into Morehardt's Cadillac Escalade and put the pigs in the back. By the following day, the pigs had crapped all over everything.

Dad won the team roping buckle in 1985. He was 50. He won the award for the fastest time when he was 62. I was 41 at the time and didn't think that was a big deal. Now that I am older and everything hurts when I wake up, I see it in a whole new light. More confirmation to the rest of us that age is just a number.

NEVER DULL!

1997

Dad was never still. He was always into something. He and Mom were alike in that regard. Both of them were at a full gallop all the time. Dad made Mom mad because he would spend his time fixing an old tractor, welding panels for the arena, or fabricating a water truck. Mom thought a better use of his time was to do surgeries, then go buy a new water truck.

RANCHEROS VISITADORES

Dad planted some two-foot-tall trees near the arena so that he could eventually have shade when they roped. The hose from the clinic wasn't long enough to reach his new trees.

He traded with one of his clients for a 1967 Chevy. Dad and the sixteen-year-old hired man, Doug Wheeler, tore off the bed of the truck and welded a flatbed on. Then Dad traded someone for a water tank. When the Tassajara Volunteer Fire Department replaced their trucks, he got some discarded fire hoses.

One of Dad's favorite sayings was, Waste not, want not. Mom's philosophy was, You can't take it with you. No hearse has ever had a trailer attached.

Mom was a clean freak, Dad tended to be a hoarder, and poor Doug was in the middle. Each May, when Dad drove out of our place for ten days for the RV Trail Ride, the next truck that came through the front gate was dropping off a dumpster. The entire time my dad was gone, Mom was doing spring cleaning and would start chucking things.

As soon as Dad pulled out, Mom told Doug to help her. She worked right beside him. He told me her stamina and strength were remarkable. She went into the tack room and drug out heavy, smelly horse blankets that got wet when the toilet backed up. She was not what he expected and was definitely not fragile or prissy.

"These have got to go." It was hot, and Doug was impressed by how fast she moved. She was a scrapper. He was not going to be outworked by a 40-year-old lady. He took the blankets from her. He tossed them in the dumpster.

175

NEVER DULL!

Doug turned around and saw Mom dragging a cart that only had three wheels to the dumpster. Doug protested, "Dr. Sharp says he is going to fix that. He is going to order a new axle and weld it together."

"That will cost more than the cart. Out it goes."

Doug rolled his eyes and threw it in the dumpster.

She came out of the tack room with an old saddle that had part of the fender ripped and was missing a stirrup.

Doug frowned. "Dr. Sharp said he's going to fix that."

"No, he's not," she said with disdain.

"He says he is going to learn leatherwork from a saddle maker."

"In his spare time? Between doing surgery and emergency calls? Nope, he can buy a new one." She slung the saddle into the dumpster.

This continued all week until she had everything spic and span.

Doug didn't mind the hard work but hated having two bosses.

Chapter 14

No Such Thing As Easy Money

Mom was made for multi-level marketing. She loved everything about it. She liked the products and competition, and hosting the meetings was a blast. There was no one better than her at throwing parties and exciting people.

Her friend said, "She could have been the next Jim Jones. She could talk anybody into drinking the Kool-Aid."

Mom was late for lunch with her girlfriends at their favorite restaurant, Father Nature's Shed, in Danville. She blew in and plopped down in the booth just as her friends were discussing the latest fad that had changed their lives. She didn't even know what they were talking about yet. Without any hesitation said, "I don't know what it is! But I know I want one!"

She tried Amway for a while, but that was too boring. I can't remember all the names, but she was involved with 32 multi-level marketing businesses.

- Water filters
- Ab stimulator machines that would work out your tummy while you watch TV

NEVER DULL!

- New Vision Minerals
- A baseball cap that would grow thicker-fuller hair
- Mangosteen
- Blue Green Algae
- Vemma
- Strap-on boots that had springs on the bottom for jogging (we got rid of those quickly because they did not come with wrist guards)
- Xango
- No-run pantyhose
- Toothbrushes
- Jewelway

And let's not forget something that started with a Q for safety when you traveled. It replaced your mace, and you could take it on the airplane. It has a siren and an electric shocker. This was available years before Tasers came out. Somebody probably modified a cattle prod and turned it into a multi-level marketing company. It was marketed as being 'totally safe.'

It wasn't.

One of the best . . . I should rephrase that, one of the worst was Cleopatra's secret! I am ashamed to admit it, but I drank the Kool-Aid too.

I have got to hand it to whoever cooked this idea up. Their marketing was flawless. Mom and I believed every word they told us. Another bonus to Mom was that I was finally excited about beauty products. All I cared about was the money.

No Such Thing as Easy Money

We believed that we were in the right place at the right time. Because it was a startup, they could not afford the expensive manufacturing machines. That's where we came in.

The special ingredient came from Europe. The secret ingredient duplicated rapidly at the correct temperature because it was a naturally occurring cell organism. And because of breakthrough research, it could be replicated and grown at home inexpensively. But it was very labor-intensive.

We prided ourselves on the fact that we were not afraid of a little hard work, and we did not mind getting our hands dirty.

Their marketing said that if you understood how cancer cells replicated, *you would understand this.* But cancer was bad, and this was good. Once the secret miracle ingredient made contact with your skin, it would reverse aging. This was going to revolutionize the beauty industry.

We were about to hit it big!

We bought 100 units and waited breathlessly for our shipment to arrive. We were so eager to get started. Then we received a very plausible and believable telegram from the company that our delivery was delayed due to customs issues.

Then we were notified by telegram again that the company was about to sell out of product because of high demand. But if we acted fast, we could increase our current order.

We decided to double our order. We reasoned, "An opportunity like this does not come along all the time. This is a once-in-a-lifetime deal. We have to get out on the ground floor before it explodes." Mom's favorite saying was, "It takes money to make money."

NEVER DULL!

Oh, one other thing, the reversing aging thing would not happen in its raw state in our garage. It had to be sent to the lab and refined. Then it would go to the Tova Borgnine skincare company. But we could buy the refined product for a discount because we were on the ground floor. All we had to do was place a pre-order now. And pay for it.

Spoiler alert. The miracle ingredient was really just sourdough starter.

We had 200 eight-ounce glasses of sour milk and yogurt in our garage. The secret ingredient would grow overnight, and we would scrape it off the top with a sterilized, specially-made scraper. Strangely, the scraper looked a lot like a wooden tongue depressor that could be bought at Walmart.

We would scrape the foam every morning and put it in special envelopes. If it wasn't growing fast enough each night, the company also sold special heat lamps and fans to keep the temperature in the specified optimal window. The company offered classes on this if you needed them. But, pffffttt. Mom and I did not need to. We were smart.

The special envelopes and the sterilized scrapers were available for purchase from Cleopatra's Secret Inc. and could be overnighted to us for a special handling fee. But we were lucky and did not have to pay that fee since we were at the gold level.

We set up a clothesline in the garage. Then we would hang up the envelopes with clothes pins to dry. Sadly, her bronze Cadillac would have to be parked outside, but this was worth it, and it would only be for a short time just until the company had enough money to buy machines.

No Such Thing as Easy Money

It took a day for the envelopes to dry, and then we would package them and send them to . . . guess where? Las Vegas. But rest assured, when the envelopes arrived, they were quality control checked and sent to Europe. Investment in the laboratory was also an opportunity reserved for special people.

We wanted to be special!

You had to be at the platinum level and be experienced in making Cleopatra's Secret before you were allowed to invest in that.

But, as Mom said, a girl can dream. It was something to aspire to . . . a long-term goal.

Long term. You know, two to three months from now.

I can't believe we did this. I used my money from riding lessons and selling horses to buy a position on Mom's downline. My deal with my mom was that as long as I did the work in the garage, she would put her friends under me.

I mean, really, as she said, it only made sense. She had way more friends who were interested in beauty than I did.

In the '80s, a Ponzi scheme made its way around the West Coast. Mom had many, many friends, and she was slightly . . . what is the right word? Gullible?

She was optimistic about everything and trusted everyone. She was full speed ahead and didn't take time to step back and investigate.

181

Never Dull!

The idea was that you would buy a position on the list, tell two friends, they would tell two friends, and so on. One, two, four, eight, sixteen. The concept was called The List, or another name was The Pyramid. You would invest $1,000 to buy a position; when the list was filled in at the bottom with 16 names, the top person would make $16,000, and the list would split.

This was so exciting!

I remember going to the supermarket and filling our cart with cookies and lemonade. We emptied the shelves of Dolly Madison oatmeal cookies. We made pots and pots of coffee because, after all, "If people are coming to a party, then we have to give them something to eat and drink."

It started out slow, or at least it was slow to Mom. She operated at a higher speed than most. She scraped together $1,000 and waited impatiently for her name to reach the top of the list. Before she left to go to a meeting, she told us, "Good things come to those who wait."

Those who wait? What are you talking about? It's been less than a week.

One night. Mom's name had reached the top of the list, and she got $16,000. When she came home, she burst in the door and threw stacks of money in the air, and the two of us rolled around in it.

Mom and Dad were friends with Wayne Hawkins. He played for the Oakland Raiders for ten years. He was a five-time AFL all-star and played in the Super Bowl in 1968 against the Packers. Wayne lived a large life and had a lot of friends!

No Such Thing as Easy Money

Mom wanted him in her downline. Mom could talk anyone into anything, but she had met her match with him. He was not going to budge but loved sparring with her. She was like a mouse, and he was the cat. He kept toying with her, but she was convinced she could get him to change his mind.

A few days passed, and Mom got really excited because "Someone got wind of a $5,000 list. Now it's big money!" In reality, somebody just made a new list and put themselves at the top. It didn't come from anywhere. They created it out of thin air.

The next day, I started a five-dollar list at school. By fifth period I got called into the principal's office and was told to cease and desist. He made me give back all the money. What a wet blanket. He ruined all my fun. I told him I was an entrepreneur, and he was squashing my passion to better myself and my friends.

He said, "Right, you will get Algebra next year, and then you will understand exponential equations. Give the money back."

Mom was in town getting her nails done, and she was talking a mile a minute about The Pyramids and how big they are and they need more room. A lady next to her wanted to be part of the excitement. She volunteered her husband's warehouse in Concord for the next pyramid party.

Fantastic!

Mom loved the party aspect of it, the more the merrier. She truly wanted everyone to have fun and honestly did not see a problem with this. In her mind, she had an unlimited amount of friends. She would never run out.

Never Dull!

The location of the meeting was all very hush-hush. You had to know someone personally to join. You would meet the person who invited you at an off-ramp on the interstate. A car with a tennis ball on the antenna would pull off, flash its lights, and the gaggle would follow it to the secret location of the Pyramid party.

Mom bought more oatmeal cookies and made more coffee. She put a tennis ball on her antenna and led the gaggle of cars to the warehouse in Concord.

I remember the utter madness of all of this. Dad had to pull the fuse on the automatic antenna on her rose-colored Cadillac to get a tennis ball on.

Now that I am older and look back, I don't think my dad knew what was going on. It all came about so quickly, and this crazy level of enthusiasm was normal behavior for Mom. He didn't notice anything unusual because she was like this all the time. As Dad said, "It is easier to let that filly run than it is to try and rein her in."

Or maybe he did try to talk to her, but Mom was so full speed ahead that she would not listen to Dad. She was so amped. A tranquilizer dart for a charging rhino would not have slowed her down.

Mom was a celebrity at The Pyramid parties because she brought so many friends who were new blood. And she found a larger venue for the wildly successful Pyramid parties. That night in Concord, she was elevated to a leadership position. She was at the front of the room, sitting at a folding table and writing people's names down. Mom brought the cookies, and an architect donated large sheets of paper. He carefully drew out The List like a great big family tree.

Once the bottom row was filled in with 16 names, the list would split. The top page would be ripped off with great fanfare and cut in half with scissors. New pieces of paper with sixteen blank lines would then be attached to the two separate lists, and the bottom row would get filled in with names.

So exciting!

Mom would write down the names, and the person next to her would take the stacks of money. Usually, $100 bills. It was bad manners to bring $20 bills. They took too long to count and slowed things down. The Pyramid parties were so popular that banks ran out of $100 bills.

At the beginning of the night, with her $16,000, Mom bought three positions on the $5,000 list and one position on the $1,000 list. The $5,000 list only had eight positions at the bottom before it would split. The top spot would receive $40,000. This meant the $1,000 she started with would become $136,000. That is big money! That is almost $600,000 in today's dollars.

Mom's name was moving up the lists and would soon be at the top. Her heart was pounding.

Just then, the doors at the back of the warehouse burst open. Several police officers came through the doors, and some were armed. A man in a windbreaker was in the audience. He jumped up, took his jacket off, and flashed his badge. He shouted, "Everyone stay seated! Nobody moves!"

The man sitting next to Mom was a lawyer in real life. He whispered to her, "Don't say anything. Keep your mouth shut."

She gasped. "But I'm not very good at that!"

"Just play dumb. You know nothing."

"Ha! Well, I am good at that!"

The police went straight to the front table and swept up all the cash. A police officer started to roll up the list, and Mom saw her name disappearing. She leaned forward and whimpered.

The lawyer elbowed her. "Zip it."

I was at home with Dad waiting up for her. Brian was peacefully asleep. I wanted to stay up and roll around in the money again. It was getting late, and Dad started to get concerned. Finally, in the wee hours, Mom drove in. She stomped up the walkway and slammed the door.

Dad asked, "I was getting worried. What happened?"

"I got arrested."

Dad's mouth fell open.

I looked at both of them. I asked, "Did this mean no money?"

Mom's Irish was up, and she was mad. "They threw me in the paddy wagon like a common criminal. They took us to the station and booked us. It was so humiliating. They went to take my fingerprints. I told them I just had my nails done. They didn't care."

Dad rubbed his head.

"Then they took our mug shots. I asked if anyone had a comb. That got a laugh, but they didn't care."

He said, "Oh dear." It was all becoming clear.

No Such Thing as Easy Money

"Then a detective interviewed me. He was so nice! I have his card. I started to give him the sales pitch about The List. He shook his head and waved his hands like he was erasing the words that came out of my mouth. He grabbed both of my hands and shook them. He said, 'Ma'am! You don't want to tell me this. I am the enemy. Silence is your friend.' He got up from the table and told his partner to kick me out of the building before I incriminated myself.

"Then they kicked us out the door. In the middle of the night! I was petrified to be turned loose in downtown Concord, but when we went outside, hundreds of people were waiting for us and cheering."

"Oh boy." Dad poured himself several fingers of whiskey.

She talked nonstop without taking a breath, "I am so late because everybody that got arrested went to an all-night restaurant to discuss our legal defense. Eleven people were arrested, and ten of us decided to join forces and hire one lawyer. One guy was an idiot; he said he would represent himself and go it alone. He got kicked out of our brainstorming session. Anyway, one guy has a golf cart business. One guy is in a band. Somebody else has an 18-wheeler with a flatbed. Another guy is in the Porta-Potty business. One of the guys has a catering business. Another guy owns a bar and an ice company. I said, Let's have a band and sell beer! You can have it at our place! We have 156 acres! Invite everyone! One guy was so negative. He said it's illegal to sell tickets to a BBQ and serve beer if you don't have a permit. I told him it's not illegal to have a party. People coming to the party can donate. I'll front the money. Everything will work out."

Never Dull!

LOCATION OF THE PYRAMID RALLY

That was the theme of Mom's life; everything always did work out. She had zero fear of consequences.

Mom didn't sleep that night. The adrenaline was pumping, and she was on the warpath. She honestly did not believe there was anything illegal about this. The whole exponential equation thing was lost on her. She brushed it aside. "That's too complex. I've got a party to plan!"

Doug, the hired man, helped get the place ready for The Pyramid Rally. He had invested $1,000 and was eager to get it back.

The day before the rally, twelve Porta-Potties were dropped off. On the morning of the big event, a beer truck arrived. A semi drove in, and the eight-person band set up on the back of the flatbed. Then the catering company brought three BBQ pits and 2,000 turkey legs.

No Such Thing as Easy Money

Dad wondered if this might be a little on the excessive side.

Mom said, "Oh don't worry. The bigger, the better. It will be great. Everything will work out."

She got arrested in July. It was hot and had not rained for weeks. Doug was told to fill three horse troughs with ice and 600 cans of Shasta soda, and 500 bottles of water. He said, "This is going to be a big party!"

It was a huge party! The Pyramid concept worked this time. They told two friends, and they told two friends, and the next thing you know, over 3,500 people came. After paying for the food and the beer, they still had $25,000 left to hire a lawyer to defend them.

The theme for The Pyramid Rally was red, white, and blue. Mom was the welcoming committee. She had an ice cream bucket with a slit on the top. As people drove in, they rolled down their windows and put cash in the bucket, she waved her tiny American flag, and they tooted their horns. Mom was so in her element.

So that I could direct cars where to park, I rode a horse with an orange reflective vest and red water ski flags. I was in my element too. I was on a horse and telling people what to do. This was great. I directed the cars to the hayfield, past the band on the flatbed, the beer tent, and the BBQ. They would park out there, and golf carts would pick up people and bring them back to the festival area. It was a giant party.

It was hot out, and her face was the same color as her red shirt. She had on white pants and a sparkly blue hat. So many cars were pulling in that dust was becoming a problem and ruining the vibe of her party. Her white pants were getting dusty. Mom shouted at Doug to get our water truck and wet down the road.

Doug brought out our 1967 Chevy flatbed with the 1,000-gallon water tank. He unrolled 20 feet of fire hose and fired up the gas-powered water pump to pressurize the tank.

As luck would have it, Wayne Hawkins pulled in driving his new blue Cadillac Fleetwood. He rolled down his window and shouted, "Hey! Jailbird! I hear you're having a party."

"Wayne, you son-a-bitch!" Her eyes flashed. She was like a woman possessed. She grabbed the firehose and sprayed him right in the face. Wayne was blown back and attempted to roll up his window, but the nozzle got wedged in the window. Mom filled his Cadillac with water.

Doug was trying to pull the hose away from her. "Mrs. Sharp, Mrs. Sharp. No!"

She was incensed. "Doug, back off, or you're fired."

Doug raised his hands in surrender and stepped back. He needed this job. He was $1,000 in debt.

A bystander turned off the water pump.

Wayne was a good sport and died laughing. When Mom saw him laughing, she came out of her trance and laughed.

Wayne opened the car door, and water rushed out and splashed on the dirt. He was soaked! He used his shirt to wipe his face. He got out of his car and hugged Mom. He said, "I'll just turn this into insurance. I'll say I was hit by a tornado, and her name was Marian!"

Doug couldn't believe the absurdity of this. He'd never seen anything like it.

No Such Thing as Easy Money

In the end, The Pyramids were ordered to cease and desist.

- Mom and the other jailbirds got acquitted. For once in her life, she kept her mouth shut.
- The guy that decided to go it alone had to do 1,000 hours of community service.
- Doug never got his $1,000 back.
- Mom and Dad never did strike it rich with The Pyramids. They lost $1,000, but they had one heck of a party.

Chapter 15

OH, THE PLACES YOU'LL GO

In retrospect, I now realize how blessed my brother and I were. We had a great life. We still believed in God but only went to church on high holidays. We were just too busy going to rodeos every weekend. We were submarine Catholics and only surfaced on Easter and Christmas Day.

We didn't have séances or Ouija boards, we weren't that nuts, but Mom was highly superstitious. She said it was because she was Irish.

To keep bad luck away, the rules were:

- No hats on the bed.
- Don't open an umbrella in the house.
- Don't walk under a ladder.
- Broken mirrors bring bad luck.
- Throw salt over your shoulder to protect yourself from evil spirits.

Trying to keep up with what I could and couldn't do was exhausting. There was much disagreement about whether the horse shoe should face up or down when nailed above the door.

Up meant the house would be protected from evil spirits. Down meant the luck would be sprinkled on anyone who came through the door. But (this is how ridiculous it was) guests would have to leave through the same door they entered because if they didn't, they would take all the good luck with them, and the house would be unprotected. So then you would have to get a new horseshoe.

And we couldn't tell the guests which door they could go out because . . . . well, if we did, they would think we were crazy.

We were also careful not to step on a crack, just in case it would break our mother's back. Since I couldn't talk back when Mom and I fought, I'd step on every crack I could find the next day.

Mom went to a psychic. If it was good enough for Nancy Reagan, it was good enough for her. The psychic told her things like her lucky dates and what colors were good and bad. Mom asked about her kids, and the psychic said, "Your son will be very successful, and your daughter is going to be a writer."

"Oh, a rider? Like a world champion?"

"No. A writer of books."

"Meh, she's not that smart."

That statement caused her to discount the wisdom of the psychic, and we moved on to astrology. She told me that my unbelief was ruining the vibe. I was too serious, and I was causing negative energy. She told me again that I should lighten up.

I would complain to my dad, "Wise up, Dad, you're letting her get away with all this crap."

"Oh, your mother. Sometimes it's easier to let that filly run. If you pull back on her, she will only go faster. She'll run out of steam someday."

"No, she won't. She's like the Energizer Bunny on crack."

So, at 16 years old, I thought I knew everything and started bossing my mother around. You can imagine how well that went. She did not like being told what to do, especially by a teenager, and particularly her daughter.

In 1982 I was a sophomore at Monte Vista High School, and I went to career day in the auditorium. Since rodeo star or horse trainer was not a box I could check, I told the counselor, "My mom wants me to be a flight attendant."

Ms. Thereet asked me, "Why not be a pilot?"

I was a typical teenager. I wrinkled my nose and said patronizingly, "I don't think they let girls do that."

"Ummm-hmmm." She smiled knowingly. "I think you should try."

Remember RSC? Roddy-Sparrowk-Cook? Jack Roddy and Jack Sparrowk sold their shares of the stock contracting company to Bob Cook. Bob had a ten-week contract for a Wild West show called the American Rodeo Show at the Mitzi Greenland Amusement Park near Fukuoka, Japan, and another six-week contract at Expoland near Osaka, which happened to be the site of the World's fair in 1970.

Before this, Bob had produced other Rodeo Shows overseas. Steve Cosca, the same guy that rode Jawbreaker, went to Belgium and Taiwan.

Importing live animals to Japan was a nightmare. Bob hired my dad and Dr. Lowell Dorius to issue veterinary health certificates for each animal and work with Japanese Customs.

A few days after I had been to career day, the rodeo stock was departing on a Flying Tigers 747 to Japan. That's how long ago it was, Flying Tigers was still in business. Eventually, they got bought out by FedEx.

FLYING TIGERS 747

Dad had to test the blood of every animal and then verify that they got on the airplane. He told me he needed an assistant and asked if I wanted to go with him. "Oh yeah! I am all over it!" I was 16 years old. I got to skip school and be with my dad.

Very early in the morning, Dad and I went to Stockton Airport in the central valley of California. It was a clear night, which meant ground fog would develop and reduce the visibility to nearly zero when the sun came up.

Portable pens were set up on the tarmac for the rodeo stock, and two cowboys were mounted on their horses. One wore a black felt hat and was rolling a smoke. He was sitting cross-legged with his knee hooked around his saddle horn. The other one with a mustache sat upright in his saddle, fast asleep.

The cowboy's horses got spooked when a tug ripped across the ramp and halted in front of the loading chute. A 50-year-old guy in a reflective vest that said LOADMASTER jumped off the tug. A piece of duct tape partially covered the word LOAD, and all that was visible was MASTER. He barked at Dad, "You the vet?"

"Yes, sir," Dad said crisply. I thought Dad might salute.

The loadmaster looked at the cowboy with the cigarette. "Put that thing out! You're gonna blow us up! We're gonna load tail first and then move forward."

The cowboy with a mustache asked earnestly, "Tail first? Like they have to go up the ramp backward?"

The other cowboy muttered, "Don't be stupid, Russ." He took a drag from his cigarette and crushed it out on the sole of his cowboy boot. He swung his leg over, tipped his hat, and said, "Let's do what the man says."

NEVER DULL!

To separate the animals, ten-foot by ten-foot pens were installed on the main deck of the 747. The lightweight calves had to go first due to weight and balance. Then the roping steers, then bucking bulls, then bucking horses, and finally, the saddle horses.

The bulls weighed about 2,500 pounds each. The loadmaster said, "The bulls with horns will go on the inside so they won't puncture the side of the airplane and cause a rapid D."

Dad questioned, "A rapid what?"

"A rapid decompression. This is a freighter, not a passenger plane. If the airplane loses oxygen, there is no rubber jungle of little margarine cups to place over your nose and mouth. A rapid D would be a disaster over the pond. Let's go. We're burnin' daylight."

Russ laughed and told the other cowboy, "Now he's talking about a jungle and a pond."

The loadmaster shouted, "Stop talkin' and start doin'! This plane better be loaded and ready to take off before the sun comes up!" He jumped back on the tug and sped away.

The cowboy with the black hat put his foot in the stirrup and said, "I'll go tell the bulls to synchronize their watches and prepare for lift-off."

What the cowboys didn't understand, and neither did I until several years later, was that several factors went into calculating the takeoff time. The airplane had to take off before the sun came up and the fog rolled in. If the airport got socked in, the fog would not burn off until the early afternoon, and by that time, the pilots would have timed out because their duty day starts when they arrive at the airport. The takeoff time was based on actual headwinds, and the landing time had to be during business hours when the Japanese Health Department was open to inspect the animals.

It was all very complex—a lot of moving parts.

The cowboys sorted the animals out of their pens and pushed them into the squeeze chute one by one. Dad did a blood test, checked the brand on their hips, and made a checkmark on the manifest. Then he signaled a cowboy to open the front gate of the chute. When the gate opened, the animal bolted forward into the narrow alley that led to a ramp. I was on foot, and my job was to keep the animals moving up the ramp and onto the airplane.

We got into a rhythm. Everything was going smoothly and running faster than we expected.

We had to stop the operation when the three pilots arrived. A set of stairs mounted on a tug was pulled up to the passenger door on the left side of the airplane. The pilots climbed up the airstairs but had to wait until the panels on the main deck could be removed to allow room for the ladder to drop down from the upper deck. To avoid getting cow poop on their shoes, the pilots stepped carefully and did not set their heavy flight bags down.

The pilots went up the steep ladder and loading the animals started up again. Each time I went up the ramp, I tried to get a peek at the cockpit on the upper deck. The captain was getting a cup of coffee from the upper deck galley and spotted me. He said, "Hey. You want a tour?" I nodded eagerly. He waved me up, "Get on up here!"

Never Dull!

I climbed the ladder and went forward to the cockpit. We chatted about the weather and the Rodeo Stock. I thought they were going straight to Japan, but the airplane would refuel in Anchorage. When it landed, the pilots would get off and go to the hotel, and fresh pilots would get on.

The co-pilot said, "So what do you want to be when you grow up?"

"I am not sure. My teacher thinks I should be a pilot."

He motioned me to sit in the left seat. He gave a running commentary as he pre-flighted and checked every knob and switch in a snake-like pattern. The captain watched with wonder as if he was seeing all this for the first time and was acting surprised at everything the co-pilot said.

The third pilot, the flight engineer, was busy flipping switches on his panel and then checking every instrument in the front of the cockpit again. I thought *That was odd. The co-pilot just went over all the switches, didn't he trust the other guy?*

The radio squealed, and a voice said, "Flying Tigers 801, clearance available, advise ready to copy."

The captain got serious and pointed his finger at me, "You, outta my seat." I got up quickly and headed for the stairs.

The captain said, "No, no. You're fine; sit in that jump seat there." He pointed to the observer's seat right behind his seat. "I'm sure our fearless co-pilot wants to impress you with his read-back skills."

The captain carefully put his cup of coffee in the cup holder, took his seat, and buckled his seat belt. I was unsure why he did that, but it looked like a mindless habit. When the buckle clicked, suddenly, the atmosphere changed; the captain was now in charge. He dug into his flight bag, got a notepad with Marriott on it, and took a pen that said Hilton out of his chest pocket. The co-pilot held the microphone to his lips and looked expectantly at the captain. The captain waved his pen like an orchestra conductor and signaled the co-pilot.

The co-pilot keyed the mic, "Flying Tigers 801, ready to copy."

Instantly, the guy on the radio started talking very fast, and all three pilots wrote down what he said.

The captain frowned. "Tell him to stand by." The flight plan was attached to a clipboard and placed face down on the glare shield. The captain grabbed the clipboard with a flourish and unclipped it. Over his shoulder, he said to me, "Now I have to do some captain shit. This is why they pay me the big bucks."

He looked at the flight plan, scribbled some numbers, and did some math. He held his pen to his lips to help him think and then shook his head. He passed the flight plan back to the flight engineer. "Check my math, will ya?" He looked over his reading glasses at the co-pilot. "We're never gonna make it. Ask for thirty-one."

I sat perfectly still. My eyes darted back and forth between the pilots. Never gonna make it? They all seemed so calm.

The co-pilot started speaking rapidly into the mic. He did not take a breath and sounded just like an auctioneer. He read back exactly the same thing the guy on the radio just said. Then he finished with, "Request three one oh."

NEVER DULL!

Instantly, the voice on the radio came back with, "Amend to Flight Level three one zero, Read back correct, have a great flight."

Suddenly, the three men were busy. The flight engineer flipped some switches on his panel, and the co-pilot finished checking everything on his side. He held a laminated checklist and waited reverently for the others to finish. The captain called for the preflight checklist. The co-pilot read it, and the other two responded crisply with serious responses. It was like a finely choreographed dance, and everyone knew their roles.

When they finished, their demeanor returned to casual and carefree.

The co-pilot asked me if I had any questions. I nervously asked, "What do you mean you're not gonna make it?"

The captain said, "To altitude. We weigh too much. My partner here is too chubby." He pointed at the co-pilot and puffed out his cheeks. "Sorry, I'm kidding. The real answer is that our fuel load is over 300,000 pounds. Our engines are most fuel-efficient at a higher altitude but are not powerful enough to get us up there right away. We have to wait until we burn off some gas and stair-step up to a higher altitude."

I nodded my head thoughtfully, like I understood what he just said.

The flight engineer asked me, "Scared yet?"

"Not yet."

The captain carefully took the lid off his coffee cup. He asked me over his shoulder, "So? What do you think about being a pilot?" He took a sip.

"This is amazing, but it looks pretty hard."

The co-pilot said, "This job is a piece of cake." He grabbed the yoke with both hands. "Pull back, and the houses get smaller; push forward, the houses get bigger. Any idiot can do it! Just look at our captain here!" The co-pilot slapped the captain on the shoulder.

The captain comically flinched and spilled coffee on his tie. He yanked off his clip-on tie and shook it off. He muttered to himself, "I get no respect around here. I tell 'ya. No respect."

I was hooked. Here they were, getting ready to fly an 800,000-pound airplane. They were serious one moment and funny the next.

The loadmaster came halfway up the stairs and shouted at the captain, "Good to go?"

"Yep." He hiked his thumb at me. "You'd better get out of here. Otherwise, you will be going with us."

I nodded and quickly headed for the stairs. "Thank you so much."

I floated down the ramp and told my dad, "I am going to be a pilot. I am gonna fly that thing someday."

I was beyond excited, and my dad had zero emotion. Dad was distracted. He absently said, "Well, isn't that nice." He was back to being cranky and concentrating on the task at hand. A blue roan bull was in the chute. I learned later that he was the lead bull, the alpha, and thought he was in charge. The bull was mad and slinging snot everywhere. My dad was watching the bull's eyes. The cowboy would open the gate as soon as the bull would look forward.

The bull kept looking back to the other bulls using his butt as a battering ram on the gate. If he had seen another bull go up the ramp, he would have followed, but he had to be forced because there was such a long break in the action. The bull bellowed and stomped his feet. Every gate rattled. He lowered his head and was getting ready to ram the front gate of the chute.

"How 'bout we load this puppy before you go trottin' all over the world? Focus, Heather, focus."

"Gotcha." I was back to being serious and doing my job.

Another bull bellowed from inside the airplane.

At the exact moment when the bull was moving forward, the cowboy opened the gate and jokingly yelled, "Charge!" The bull's forward motion propelled him up the ramp and into the airplane. As he trotted up the ramp, the bull mooed to his buddy.

When the bull got into the plane, we could hear a gate clang shut behind him like the sound a prison door would make. My dad and I looked at each other and winced. These bulls were used to freedom, and now they were being confined.

Next were the bucking horses, followed by the saddle horses. The bucking horses were eager. When the gate opened, they were off like a shot and ran up the ramp. Next were the saddle horses. They were more apprehensive and had to be coaxed.

Unfortunately, these animals would never make it back to the States. They had a one-way ticket to Japan and would end up on somebody's plate.

The last horse to be loaded was called Dynamite. He was over 16 hands tall, dark bay with a blaze and four white stockings. He would be used to carry the American flag during the grand entry and as a pickup horse during the bronc riding.

He was gorgeous. He held his head high and strutted up the ramp. A cowboy put him in the last pen on the main deck and shut the gate. Dynamite looked down at the cowboys, my dad and me, and all the workers on the ramp. It was like he was a world ruler or a rock star saying farewell to his adoring fans.

Dad and I heard the whine of the hydraulic pump as the nose cone was lowered and saw Dynamite peeking around the corner of the fuselage and looking at the landscape for one last time.

In Japan, as well as France, horse meat is on the menu. Dad read my mind. He said, "Don't think about it, Heather. Focus on what you can control."

We watched the airplane taxi out. It paused for a minute to do what I now understand was the pre-takeoff checklist. Then it taxied into position on the runway. The noise was earsplitting as the engines spooled up. Behind the airplane, the grass lay down because each of the four engines produced 44,000 pounds of thrust.

When the airplane started its takeoff roll, a mist began to develop because of the heat from the engines. The airplane's weight moving through the still air caused wing-tip vortices to form that looked like horizontal tornadoes. The airplane broke ground just as the sun rose.

Dad put his arm around my shoulder and said, "So that's gonna be you someday, huh?"

"Without a doubt."

Never Dull!

"You're just like your mother."

"What?"

"Relax, Heather. It's a compliment. You are not going to let anything stand in your way."

Chapter 16

FAIRY TALE OR TRUTH?

I heard the following story secondhand from a cowboy who knew one of the cowboys on the flight. He was telling this story at a party where lots of whiskey was flowing. Everything else in this book is true, but I question if this story really happened.

Before you read on, do you know the difference between a fairy tale and a cowboy story? The fairy tale starts out "In a beautiful land far, far away." And the cowboy story starts out, "No shit, this really happened."

The two cowboys, the one with the black hat and Russ with the mustache were the last to board the airplane and sat in the first-class seats on the upper deck. They were going with the rodeo stock to the amusement park and would be the pickup men during the bronc riding at the Wild West show.

NEVER DULL!

While the airplane got fuel in Anchorage, the cowboys got a cab to a liquor store nearby and drank on the way to Japan.

When they landed at Fukuoka Airport, the animals had been traveling for over 18 hours. Before that, they had been in quarantine for eight hours, and then it took four hours to load the airplane.

When the airplane landed, the cowboys were no help at all. They were able to stumble down the airstairs, climb into a cargo van, and fall back asleep. They were suffering from jet lag and brown-bottle disease. When they woke up, the animals were gone. The cowboys cleared customs and went outside to the curb. They did not have to find an interpreter to get a cab to take them to the amusement park; their cowboy hats told the cab driver all he needed to know.

I don't know the details of how the animals got off the airplane, but I imagine the Japanese ground crew led Dynamite down the ramp, and every other animal was so worn-out and dehydrated that they just followed the leader like little lambs.

I am curious to know if they had halters on hand for the 1,800-pound bucking bulls and the 400-pound roping steers and how they got them on. That part is a mystery. They may have constructed the halters out of rope right there to make a custom fit for each animal.

I envisioned five Japanese men in white suits with hard hats and muck boots surrounding each bull and yelling at each other that they had a better idea of how to solve the problem while the bulls waited patiently. I bet the bulls had their eyes half-closed like an early-morning newscaster who snoozes in the makeup chair while her hair is done.

The amusement park had constructed individual stalls out of concrete blocks. The picture below is not an actual photo, but what I imagine the stalls looked like.

Every animal had a halter on and was cross-tied in the individual U-shaped stalls with no gate. The rodeo stock were treated like celebrities. They had belly-high shavings and the finest food. Three Japanese caretakers were assigned to each animal to care for their every need, whose previous job was massaging the muscles of cattle for Kobe beef. The animals drank gallons and gallons of water and were given a warm, high-calorie bran mash with vitamins, minerals and grain.

The Japanese caretakers had been massaging the bucking bulls and were impressed by how quickly the bulls *came back to life.*

It didn't take very long for one bull to decide he was done being tied up. He walked straight forward and snapped the crossties like they were dental floss. The caretakers started rushing around and grabbing the halters. The waving and screaming frightened the bucking horses, who reared up, broke the cross ties, and got loose. The saddle horses also got loose, except for Dynamite. He was non-plussed by the mayhem.

The rodeo stock was now running wild. If the Japanese caretakers had not tried to catch the rodeo stock right away, everything would have been fine. Given enough time, the animals would have calmed down and returned to their yummy bran mash and more water.

Bulls and horses have excellent eyesight, and they are very smart. They are creatures of habit. Bucking Bulls go to different rodeo arenas all across the US. They know the drill: Buck the cowboy off, the crowd goes wild, run around the arena and snort a few times, threaten the rodeo clown, then a gate in the arena opens, go through the gate, and it's all over until the next rodeo.

Two minutes of excitement followed by days of boredom. Like international flying, the takeoff and landing are thrilling, but the ten hours in between are mind-numbing. I speak from experience. Fourteen years after the airplane took off from Stockton Airport, I was hired to fly the 747 for Northwest Airlines.

As we know, it's usually not the crime that gets people in trouble; it's the cover-up. The caretakers wanted to secure all the animals before the cowboys woke up. More caretakers were called in the gate was opened at the end of the stables.

The blue roan bull saw the gate open, which sparked a memory of being in a rodeo arena. The bull charged towards the gate. He did not intend to flatten the several caretakers on his way out. He just did what he was trained to do, and his buddies followed him. The bucking horses did not want to be left behind and stampeded through the gate too.

That gate led to the amusement park.

Families pushing strollers and little children with ice cream cones were now running for their lives in front of the stampeding herd. It was worse than a Godzilla movie.

The cab dropped the cowboys off just in time. The one in the black hat threw a saddle on Dynamite, cinched him up, and jumped on. Russ ran to get lariats and a bridle from the shipping container. As Dynamite galloped by, Russ grabbed the saddle horn with one hand and swung up behind the cowboy with the black hat. They rode double into the amusement park. After a brief search, they found the herd milling around the food court.

Russ was dropped off at a picnic table. The cowboy on Dynamite herded some saddle horses past the table. Russ roped one of the saddle horses, put a bridle on and jumped on bareback. The cowboy on Dynamite roped the roan bull and drug him back to the stable. That bull was the Alpha, and the other animals followed.

The people in the amusement park had never seen anything like this. Ever.

The local news showed the chaos live on TV, and a wealthy Japanese businessman saw Dynamite and knew he had to have such a regal animal as a pet. He contacted the Rodeo Show producer and negotiated the purchase of Dynamite with the caveat that the horse would *work* until the run of the Rodeo Show was over.

Never Dull!

Every night before the grand entry, Dynamite had his hair and makeup done. He was dusted from head to tail with fine glitter by the cowgirl who rode him and carried the American flag. They galloped around the arena and slid to a stop in the center, the lights went dim, and a spotlight lit up Dynamite while the song "I'm proud to be an American" played. "

This picture is an actual picture of Bob Cook's wife, Nancy, in Osaka, Japan.

My aunt Nancy takes credit for their happy marriage too. She introduced them at the Livermore Rodeo in 1958.

Nancy Cook, Osaka Japan 1982

Chapter 17

You Just Can't Make This Up

Everyone's favorite story about my mom is the inversion boots story. At the time, she was about 45 years old, and we lived on Tassajara Road. The house was on a hill and overlooked the vet clinic, the roping arena, and the horse barns my dad built. Everything he ever wanted was all right there. Dad's commute to work was to walk down the hill every morning with his cup of coffee, followed by his faithful dog, Molly. What a life.

At the time, I was studying for an FAA written test. One of the statements was, *To avoid catastrophic engine failure, do not exceed the red line or operate the engine in the red arc for extended periods of time.*

I thought, *HA! Mom is in the red arc 100% of the time. Eventually, that engine is going to crap out.*

Mom liked to squeeze the maximum she could into each day. She was into every healthcare trend imaginable, and it was even better if it was combined with multi-level marketing. Hence, the Gravity Inversion Boots.

Never Dull!

She had chronic back problems, and inversion boots would be the answer to so many problems. It involved a bar that resembled a chin-up bar installed in a door jamb and padded ankle cuffs with inverted hooks. She would strap these boots to her ankles, grab the bar, kick her feet up like an acrobat, and hang upside down.

What a concept. Here's the sales pitch. It would be good for your back, make you skinnier, grow your hair faster, and make you smarter.

This contraption would stretch your back and elongate your spine. Not only would you feel better but your clothes would fit better, and you would appear skinnier. Everyone knows the same weight on a taller frame equates to a lower body mass index.

Maybe if you hung upside down long enough on that thing, you would go from being morbidly obese to an Olympic athlete.

Another marvelous benefit was that hanging upside down would send more blood to your head. Your hair would grow thicker and fuller, and you would be smarter.

After hearing the entire story you will really question if it made you smarter.

Mom was naturally pretty, but her beauty regimen took a lot of time and a lot of work. She heard that mayonnaise was a great conditioner for your hair, and if it was heat activated, it even worked better. She put a cup of mayo on her head, wrapped it with saran wrap, and used the hairdryer to heat it up.

You Just can't make this up

On her face, she smeared a mud mask made with blue-green algae. I have got to take a little detour here to tell you about the blue-green algae. It came from Tule Lake on the California/Oregon border. After the snow melts in spring, a 13,000-acre lake would appear. In the heat of the summer, algae would grow, and the lake would evaporate. It was naturally occurring and organic . . . in more ways than one.

The algae was all-natural, low-cost, and high-margin. This was made for multilevel marketing. They just had to figure out how to market it and create demand. The algae was harvested for its skin care and medicinal properties.

What Mom didn't want to hear was that the shallow lake where the algae grew was also a national wildlife refuge, and hundreds of thousands of waterfowl stopped here on their migration to Alaska. You can see where I am going with this.

Algae might not have been the only thing she was smearing on her face. The company also recommended ingesting it. But said she, "I just can't do it. It tastes like shit."

Back to the inversion boot story.

As the mask dried, it would crack and pull all the impurities out of your skin. Your face would feel like a baby's butt.

She feared the mayo and the mask would get her jammies dirty and reasoned it was much smarter to do it naked because she was going to take a shower right after, and "Why waste time?" After all, she was very busy and had a lot to do.

She was about to strap on her boots when suddenly, she thought of something. *Oh wait. They said an egg too.* She removed the saran wrap, ran naked to the kitchen, and cracked an egg on her head. As she ran back to the bathroom, she smushed it all together.

She got back to her sink and picked up the saran wrap. She did her best Nolan impersonation and, in a sing-song voice, said, "Waste not, want not." She tried to pull the saran wrap apart, but it stuck to itself. And that was taking too much time. "Oh, screw it!" She balled it up and threw it in the trash can.

She set the timer for her mask, put the boots on, and swung up like a little gymnast, and hung upside down like a bat while the blue-green algae mask began to harden. Her face would start to crack soon. She reasoned that this would be an excellent time to meditate and relax.

Ya, that's an oxymoron right there. Mom relaxing.

Ding. The timer went off.

She tried to swing up, but her back went out. "AGGGHHHH!"

She said out loud to herself, "I can do anything. Mind over matter." She took a deep breath and tried to sit up again. "AGGGHHHH!" The pain was just too much.

She spied the phone on Dad's side of the bed. The phone was too far out of reach, but she saw the cord behind the wicker basket. She took a deep breath, Swinging. Swinging, Swinging. She got up enough momentum to grab the cord and pull the phone to her.

On the rotary dial phone, she dialed the clinic. She was frustrated by the big numbers. "Why do we have this stupid antique phone? Next time push-button!"

You Just Can't Make This Up

The secretary, Terri Burnett, answered, "Danville Large Animal Clinic, may I help you?"

Mom said sweetly, "Hello, Terri, this is Mrs. Sharp. Could you send Dr. Sharp up right away?" Even in distress, she was still classy.

Terri said, "Doctor Sharp went on a farm call. He will be back any minute."

"OK, send him up the second he gets back. I really need help."

Terri said, "Shall I send Doug up to help you?"

She shouted, "No!" She collected herself. "Sorry. I mean, no, thank you. Just send Nolan up as soon as possible."

Mom hung upside down, waiting. And waiting. And waiting. Catastrophic images started to fill her head. If she couldn't get up, she would die here. The kids would come home from school and find her bloated, naked body hanging upside down.

So there she was upside down, naked, and afraid.

She started to panic. She grabbed the phone again. "Terri. Where the hell is Nolan!"

"He's not back yet!'

"Send someone up immediately!"

Terri was frantic because of the sound of Mom's voice. "Should I call 911?"

"There's no time!"

Terri saw the UPS man come in, "Can you go help Mrs. Sharp?"

Mom heard this and shouted, "Tell him the door is open!" She grabbed two magazines and strategically placed them to conceal her privates.

Two minutes later, the UPS man tentatively opened the front door, "Mrs. Sharp?"

"In here!

He came into the bedroom and tilted his head sideways. "You guys into S and M?"

"My back's out. I can't move."

He looked behind the door. "Am I on Candid Camera?"

Mom started to laugh and then winced. "Don't make me laugh. Just close your eyes and get me off of here."

"You just can't make this shit up."

"I know," she lamented, "I hear that a lot."

Dad got quite a few free horses from his clients. They couldn't pay their vet bill and wanted the horse to have a good home. Dad would fix them up and then give the horse to me.

I trained the horses that Dad got and then sold them. I made a lot of money, and the horse went to a good home. Right after the Flying Tigers airplane took off, I began saving my money for flying lessons. It took a long time, 20 months before I had enough money to start flying.

As I write this, I acknowledge that my mom was right when she told me I was ungrateful. I did not appreciate it, and I should have. I was making money because I had no expenses except my entry fees. I did not have a vet bill, feed bill, or horseshoeing bill. I didn't pay for the truck, or the gas, or the trailer, or the horses.

Like all teenagers, I thought I knew everything and was a pain in the butt. Except, I was a high achiever. I was a colossal pain in the butt. I had been telling her what to do and had been behaving like her parent since I was 16 years old. Mom and I had some tough times when we didn't talk to each other. I was not an easy kid to raise.

When I was young, I did some idiotic stuff. My first solo was in the pattern at Concord Airport. I did a few touch and goes. It was plain vanilla and non-eventful.

The next flight, however, was a little more exciting; I called Mom and told her she should keep an eye out and that I would fly by our house. My mom and brother got bed sheets and arranged them on the lawn to spell the word "Hi." They saw a tiny spec coming their way. The speck got larger and was coming right at them. Instead of waving hello, they flailed their arms and frantically screamed 'UP! UP! UP!" I think my mom was exaggerating when she says that the bedsheets blew off the lawn when I flew over. She was always so dramatic.

I buzzed my Uncle Jimmy's house once, and he called my mom to tell her I needed to see a dentist.

"Why?"

"Because she was so close, I saw she has a filling loose."

Never Dull!

Mom threw a party for my High School graduation. She was very good at throwing parties, that was for sure. She said this in front of a bunch of people, so I don't know if she was saying it for the laughs or if she really meant it.

"Heather, we have a surprise for you! Your dad and I have talked about it. For graduation, we are going to give you . . . "

She paused with dramatic anticipation.

My face lit up. I knew what was coming next.

"Boobs!"

My face fell. "Aw, I wanted flying lessons."

She patted me on the head, "Eh, we think the boobs will get you further."

As a freshman in college, I gained 15 pounds and was always tired. I came home for Christmas and had to wear sweats because I couldn't fit into the cute clothes that Mom had bought me. Mom couldn't wrap her head around the idea that I had lied to her when I said, "I exercise all the time. I only eat celery and boiled chicken breast. I just can't lose weight! It's not my fault!"

Yeah, right.

My parents thought my weight gain and fatigue were unusual. Gee, hasn't the same thing happened to every single freshman girl in the history of mankind?

My dad said, "I know what it is! You have a thyroid problem." He went to the veterinary clinic and got some

Thyroxine. "Here, take 10 MG per day. You'll feel better in no time."

I returned to college, and within a week, I was a new person. The pounds were melting off. I had non stop energy. I was cleaning my car and vacuuming at three in the morning. I cleaned my bathroom like three times.

Strangely though, I wasn't able to study. I was just too hyper.

I went to the health center at school and took my medication to show to the doctor. He examined the label, looked over the top of his glasses and scowled, "Get your dad on the phone."

Uh-oh. I called the clinic and Terri got Dad on the phone. I sheepishly handed the handset to the Doctor.

"The dosage you gave your daughter is for a 1,500-pound person."

"Oh shoot, that's the dosage for a horse. Must have been a typo."

After a few days, when the drugs wore off, I slept for three days.

Chapter 18

COME FLY WITH ME

In 1989 Mom's nest had been empty for two years, and she was getting bored. She wanted some excitement. She had been telling people, "You can do anything! Age is just a number!" It was time for her to walk the walk and lead by example.

Remember the story of when my mom was nine years old and met the flight attendant? Forty years later, she realized her dream.

At 49 years old, she became the oldest flight attendant American Airlines had hired at that point.

And who wouldn't hire her? She was cute, she was trendy, and she had a great personality. She was everything American Airlines was looking for.

Because I was hard-headed and didn't want anyone telling me what to do, I paid for most of my college. Dad sent me some money on the side, but I was not supposed to tell my mom.

NEVER DULL!

Between my junior and senior years, I had to take some time off because I was out of money. Conveniently, my mom was away pursuing her dream of being a flight attendant, and I could come home and live for free.

Mom went to training for six weeks in Dallas. American Airlines flew Dad and me first class to see Mom's graduation ceremony from training. She did it! She was so excited.

FLIGHT ATTENDANT - 1989

After training, she would be based in Washington, DC, and must fly out of three airports: Washington National, Dulles, and Baltimore. She got an apartment with two other flight attendants, Melissa and Tonette, in Alexandria, Virginia.

She made a list of all the things she wanted from home. She said it was like she was going to college and furnishing her dorm room. So much to think about. We talked about the logistics of all of this. I said, "Mom, just rent a car month to month. You will be based in San Fran in no time."

"NO!" She insisted, "I do not want a rental. I don't know how it's been maintained. It probably smells like smoke. I have to have my Cadillac."

Dad paid me to drive her car across the country. I went to Baltimore airport to pick her up from her very first trip. She was coming back from Aruba on a 767.

I was waiting for her right outside of customs. The flight crew were the last ones out. Even after an international flight, she was still effervescent. She hugged everyone goodbye. Every single flight attendant told me, "We LOVE your mom."

I took her suitcase and said, "Good to see you. We're parked over this way."

She hugged me and whispered, "Good, get me out of here! I want to get outside and kiss the ground. Oh my gosh, Heather, see that pilot? That is Captain Kangaroo. He bounced that airplane so hard I thought the masks would come down." She waved enthusiastically to him and threw a kiss, "Bye-bye!"

She was talking a mile a minute. I heard her say something about *reserve* and that she needed to call crew

FIRST TRIP TO ARUBA - 1989

scheduling before 6 PM to find out if she had been assigned a trip for tomorrow.

Then she was off to the races; she was talking non stop. She was telling me about the layover, and the passengers and the other flight attendants and then . . .

I started to glaze over and thought, *I recognize this behavior. This is how I felt when I took 1,500 pounds of thyroid medicine. But this level of excitement is natural for her.*

She told me, "At American Airlines, the flight attendants bid for positions on the airplane based on seniority. The lead flight attendant works first class and is in charge of the whole plane. That's position number one, and sometimes it goes very junior because the senior flight attendants don't want the headache of customs and immigration on an international flight. Number two is in coach, and number three assists the lead in first class. And the other seven flight attendants are in coach.

"I like number three! I'm not in charge, but I am in first class! I don't want to be in coach with the masses." Mom was a new hire and wasn't senior enough to hold position number three but would pay other flight attendants to switch with her.

She made $1,056 per month before taxes. Clearly, she was not doing this job for the money.

By now, I was driving her car across the Woodrow Wilson Bridge. She had not stopped talking. "On the way down to Aruba, I couldn't open the wine bottle. So I asked a passenger if he would help me. He did."

I laughed, "Of course he did. You can get anyone to do anything."

"On the flight back to Baltimore, a passenger rang his call button and said, 'I have a bad potato.' I picked it up and spanked it. 'Bad potato! Bad Potato!'"

"Seriously? You did that?"

"I did. It was so funny. I love this job."

I could see now why my dad was so enamored with her. She was funny. I missed her.

There was a major car wreck ahead. We came to a complete stop in the middle of the bridge. Like all the other cars around me, I turned the engine off. I glanced at my watch —5:45 p.m.

I gave her the time-out signal to silence her for a sec. "Mom? Don't you have to call American before six?"

"Shit!" She slapped the dashboard and was finally quiet. She sat there and stewed. "I wish we had a plow truck. We'd push em' out of the way."

I was trying to think of a solution. I drummed my fingers on the steering wheel and said, "It's too bad we don't have one of those car phone things."

She pointed a finger in the air and dug in her purse.

"Uh-oh." I said, "You have an idea. This can't be good.

She out got ten dollars and two miniature bottles of rum out of her purse. She opened the car door and hopped out. I could see her waving the money in the air as she went up and down the lanes of cars. "Ten dollars for a car phone! I need to make a call. Ten bucks! Anybody?"

She came back. "No one has a car phone." She plopped down in the passenger seat and slammed the car door. "I'm going to get fired if I miss this call." She crossed her arms and stared ahead. She looked so forlorn. I felt bad for her.

Mom jumped when someone knocked on her window. It was the trucker from the semi next to us. She rolled down the window and smiled cheerfully at him. He said, "I saw your dilemma. I don't have a car phone, but I used my CB. A guy in a red semi about ten cars back has a cell phone. He will let you use it."

And with that, she was gone. Not a word to me. The trucker had to step back so he could get out of her way. She ran as fast as she could in her tight uniform skirt and high heels.

The trucker looked at me and shrugged, "And I thought I'd seen everything." I shook my head and saw her redhead disappearing in the rearview mirror.

When she got there, the truck driver in the red semi leaned over and opened the passenger door for Mom. She climbed up into the truck. She was back to chipper and excited, and he was laughing at her. Everyone had this reaction to her. No one could believe how bubbly and cute she was.

He handed her the phone.

She said, "Oh shoot! I don't have my glasses. Can you dial for me?"

She gave him the phone number to Crew Scheduling. He handed the phone back to her. She put the *back side* of the phone up to her ear. In her defense, she was very excited, it was dark, and she had never used a cell phone before. She could hear it faintly ringing.

The trucker said, "Ma'am... Ma'am. It's a cell phone. You have to turn it around."

"Oh! Right!" She spun around in her seat and faced the other direction.

He tapped on her shoulder, "No, no . . . Turn *it* around." He made a twisting motion with his hand.

"Oh! Right!"

She got through to scheduling, and they told her she had no assignment for tomorrow. All was good. She gave the trucker the money and the miniatures and climbed down out of the truck.

The accident was starting to clear. The cars around me began to start their engines.

"Uh-oh," I said. All the cars started to move forward. There was nowhere for me to pull off on the side. I crept along as slowly as possible.

I said to myself, "How am I going to explain this to my dad? I had her in my clutches for one hour, but then she ran off with a trucker. Now she's somewhere in Virginia on the open road."

Just then, I could see her little redhead bobbing up and down. The cars were starting to move faster. She took off her high heels and started to run. A car honked at me to move. She stopped and banged his hood with her fist. She shouted, "EVERYBODY STOP! I have to get to my daughter."

All the cars stopped. She sprinted forward. Jumped in the car and said sweetly, "Okay, we can go now."

NEVER DULL!

Right after Mom died, Bill McCulloch called to tell me this story. Bill was a salesman for the drug company that would later become Merck Animal Health. One of the veterinary offices he called on was my dad's Danville Large Animal Clinic.

In 1989, he was 42 years old and traveled all over the US for his work. On a hot July day, he was in Arlington, Texas, at a training meeting on the second floor of the Hilton Hotel overlooking the pool.

It was day three of the training session. Bill and five other salesmen were stuck inside a stuffy meeting room. During the break, they said to each other, "Just one more hour of this, and then it is Miller time."

(Side note to the reader - they are not having a Bud Light!)

They did their best to look like they were hanging on every word the speaker said, but they were starting to fall asleep. A salesman near the window saw some very attractive young ladies come down to the pool. He nudged the guy next to him and pointed. Now everyone on that side of the room was wide awake and rubbernecking the girls in the pool.

The meeting finally ended, and they were all free to go. They looked out the window at the pool. One salesman figured, "Those girls must be poor. They can't afford much material for those swimsuits!"

Bill was the old fart of the group. He rolled his eyes, stood up, and looked thru the Venetian blinds to have a gander. The hotel just happened to be the same hotel American Airlines used as a layover hotel, and those girls were flight attendants.

There was a slightly older woman in the shallow end. She was actually 49 years old but still looked darn good. She was doing her own version of water aerobics. Occasionally she would stop at the edge and take a swig out of a coffee cup that said, Hilton. Bill squinted his eyes and said, "I bet that's not coffee that she's drinking."

The younger salesmen in the room were talking amongst themselves, deciding how they would put the hustle on those girls.

Bill looked closer at the redhead and thought, "Holy crap! I know her. That's Dr. Sharp's wife!" He stood back, put his thumbs under his belt, and hoisted up his pants over his middle-aged beer belly. He told the others, "While you young bucks figure out what to say, why don't you stand back and let a professional handle this."

He popped in a breath mint and headed for the door.

The salesmen rushed back to the window and saw Bill walking toward the pool. By now, all the girls were drying themselves off and positioning the lounge chairs for sunbathing. They were snacking on the mixed nuts and the leftover cheese tray from first class. One Flight Attendant refilled the coffee cups with the wine they had also taken from First Class.

In the meeting room, the salesmen watched Bill nod 'Hello' to all the girls. The girls politely grinned and turned their backs. One guy said, "And he goes down in flames." The salesmen all high-fived each other.

NEVER DULL!

Bill walked over to the redhead and started talking to her. "I don't know if you remember me, but I know your husband. I am here at a training meeting."

She smiled up at him. "Oh, hello there. I don't remember you, but if you are a friend of his, you are a friend of mine."

"I don't know if you are up for this, but five guys are up there in that room looking out the window and salivating over all of you. I want to pull a prank on them."

Without hesitation, she said, "This sounds fun. Let's give them something to talk about!"

She gestured for him to sit down, then sat in his lap and hand-fed him almonds. She held the coffee cup to his lips for him to take a swig and hollered for the other girls to gather around. One flight attendant even gave him a smooch and twirled his hair with her finger.

The guys went wild. They rushed down to the pool. As they approached, one flight attendant looked down her nose disdainfully, "Oh please. Go away. Big Daddy is the only thing we need."

Chapter 19

WHAT A GAL!

Because Mom had been in training and then got based in Washington DC, Dad had not seen Mom for almost three months. Right before he flew out to visit her, he said, "It has been so long . . . I am not sure I will recognize you."

She was saucy. She told him, "I will be the one with the rose between my teeth."

Mom's roommates were 25 and 28 years old. They were drinking wine together with napkins that said, "I should stop drinking, but I'm no quitter." They poured her another glass of wine and hatched a plan to make this a trip that Nolan would never forget. Knowing Mom, it did not take much persuasion.

Melissa said, "You should meet Nolan at the gate in your trench coat with nothing on underneath."

Mom thought this sounded like a great idea. They poured her some more wine, and Tonette said, "I'll go get your trench coat and high heels!" Tonette is a stinker. She hid aluminum foil in the lining of the trench coat.

Never Dull!

The roommates dropped Mom off and circled around to watch the comedy show that would soon take place. Mom tried to go through the metal detector in her trench coat and high heels.

Beep.

"Oh shoot," she patted her pockets. "Sorry, I forgot my gum." She handed the gum to the security screener and tried again.

Beep.

"Ma'am, you'll have to take your coat off and run it thru the X-ray machine."

She clutched her coat tightly around her neck. "NO! I can't take off my coat!"

"Sure you can."

"No!"

"Well then, I am sorry. You can't come through. Next."

Mom stomped away to formulate Plan B. She was determined. After all, she was no quitter.

Dad got first class from San Francisco to Washington, DC. He made friends with the couple sitting next to him and told them they had to meet his wife.

The flight attendants on that flight made sure his glass was always full. He was pretty tipsy when he got off the airplane. He looked around the gate area, but there was no Marian. "Hmmm. Well, maybe she's down at baggage claim." The other couple was really looking forward to meeting his wife. Dad had talked so much about her and was clearly very in love.

Mom knew he would come outside eventually, so she waited behind the poles. Dad came out to the curb with his new friends from first class.

"Yooo- hooo! Nolan!" She ran from pole to pole, flashing Dad.

Dad was a little tipsy and did not see her. Mom ran and flashed again. This time she stomped and screamed his name, "Nolan!"

The woman said, "I think a redhead is trying to get your attention."

The man said, "You are the luckiest man ever. This is the stuff dreams are made of."

After six months of working as a flight attendant and living in Washington, DC, Mom had had enough. She told her friend Leslie, "It was fun for a while, but I really don't like waiting on people. I like to be waited on."

She was on reserve and getting crappy trips. She was not going to Aruba and Barcelona anymore. She was going to Akron and Bismarck. And they were calling her at 3:30 in the morning to take a flight out at 6 a.m. No, thank you. She quit. She drove her car home across the country and stopped at spas and hot springs along the way.

Mom and Dad's good friends, Don and Betty Steely, were having a big party on Friday night. They lived two hours east of Danville, on my mom's route home. The plan was that Dad and I would drive together, and she would meet us there. Betty also invited Mom's brother Jimmy and sister-in-law Mae to spend the night.

Dad and I got to the party early. He was very eager to see her. He was like a kid waiting for Santa to arrive and could not take his eyes off the front door. I was getting older and for the first time, began to see them as adults rather than my parents. I was amused by how excited Dad was to get his wife back.

After the party got started and everyone had a few drinks, Mom finally arrived. Hugs and kisses all around.

Mom told stories and relived all her exciting days as a flight attendant. She was on a high, the center of attention, and everyone was laughing. Dad was so enamored. He had a silly grin and shook his head at her stories. I was watching him watching her. It was so cute.

I remember thinking, *How sweet to be that in love with someone after all these years?*

Betty told Dad that once the guests cleared out, he and Mom could have their king-size bed because he was a big guy and won't be comfortable in a dinky bed. She and Don would go to the extra bedroom. I would sleep on the couch. Jimmy and Mae would be in the guest bedroom.

While Mom was telling stories, Dad went to Mom's car and brought in her suitcase. He caught Mom's eye as he walked to the master bedroom. He raised his eyebrows and nodded like, follow me. Mom ignored him. Mom kept talking and launched into yet another tale.

Dad's shoulders slumped, and he trudged to the bedroom. Poor Dad.

WHAT A GAL!

Dad made another drink and sat by the fireplace while Mom entertained everyone with her stories. I saw Dad give her the high sign again. He hiked his thumb and pointed to the bedroom. It was past midnight, and the other guests started going home.

Finally, Mom said good night. More hugs and kisses all around.

Jimmy, Mae and I were helping Betty and Don clean up. I was loading the dishwasher and asked Jimmy if he got a look at Dad. Jimmy said, "He looked so brokenhearted. Like a kid outside an ice cream store on a hot day with no money."

Mom and Dad had been in the room for MAYBE five minutes. Jimmy thought it would be fun to go in and kiss them good night and tuck them in.

Outside the master bedroom door, we lined up like a train with our hands on the person in front of us. Jimmy was in the lead, and then the rest of the conga line. We were giggling. Before Jimmy turned the knob, he said, "Shussshhhh! Be vewrry vewrry quiet. We're hunting wabbits."

Don made a comment about what those wabbits might be doing. Jimmy said, "Nah, it's too soon." We giggled again, and the choo-choo moved forward on our tiptoes.

The last person in the conga line flicked on the light. My mom, over my dad's shoulder, waved to us and said, "Ohhhh Helloooooo."

Jimmy was horrified and yelled, "Heather! Close your eyes!" He was repelled, flew back, and took all of us down with him. We were rolling on the ground, dying laughing.

Never Dull!

Betty was crawling around on her hands and knees. "I have to gouge my eyes out with a spoon."

Mom and Dad were howling with laughter. The choo-choo crawled out of there. Don said, "Nolan didn't even slow down. It didn't even phase him."

The next morning, Betty, who is very crafty with a glue gun and glitter, made Dad a buckle out of a pie plate and aluminum foil. She presented it to him at breakfast with a certificate that said, "Don't call him a cowboy 'til you've seen him ride."

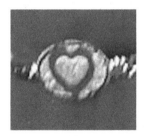

In 1993, I was a pilot for American Eagle in New York. Mom said New York sounded like fun, and she wanted to come for a visit. We were back to talking at that point. She used my travel passes and went non-rev from San Francisco to New York. Non-rev means that my family travels for free if a seat is available.

I was waiting for her at the gate at JFK. She was the very last person off and looked a little haggard after the long flight. When she saw me, she perked up. I hugged her and took her suitcase.

WHAT A GAL!

A key part of this story is that suitcase was standard issue to all the American Airlines Flight Attendants.

She said. "Good to see you. This will be fun! What will we do first? I want to go to Canal Street and buy a fake purse. I want to go to Central Park. Then I want to go to a play."

"All of this in one day? Or do you want to have pizza and go to sleep?"

"Oh no! I am ready to go downtown."

"All right. Well, we have got some options then. We could drive, but parking is twenty dollars per hour, or we could take the subway. But the subway is dangerous."

Just then, the flight crew got off the airplane. I noticed my mom was turning her back and looking intently into her purse. She was usually so friendly to absolutely everyone. She was avoiding eye contact with them and acting a little cagey. One of the flight attendants whispered to the other and gestured toward Mom. She said, "That's the one."

I started to become concerned. I asked Mom, "What's going on?"

"Oh my gosh, Heather! You are just not going to believe this. Let's walk. I have to find a bathroom!" While we walked to the bathroom, Mom explained that the gate agent gave her a seat prematurely in San Fransisco. Mom was so excited because she got the very last seat on the airplane. It was a DC-10, and Mom was all the way in the back. Moments before they shut the door, a paying passenger showed up.

Mom was about to stow her suitcase and sit down when the gate agent got on the PA, "Marian Sharp, please gather your belongings and come to the boarding door."

NEVER DULL!

"Oh Heather, I was so humiliated. I got my suitcase, and I am schlepping up to the front. Everyone is staring at me. It was so terrible. It's like I didn't pay for my ticket."

"But Mom . . . you didn't pay. You got your seat for free."

"Anyway," she flicked her hand and dismissed that comment, "So here I am, dragging my bag up the aisle, and a pilot was deadheading. He looked at my suitcase and said, You're a flight attendant right? She stood up straighter and said, Why, yes . . . I am. The pilot shrugged and said, Just take the flight attendant jumpseat.'"

My eyes narrowed. I didn't like where this story was going.

She said, "The gate agent was stressed out and wanted to get the flight out on time. The pilot jumped up, stowed my bag overhead, and told the gate agent, 'We're all good. She'll ride the jumpseat.' "So the gate agent closes the boarding door, and I go back to the aft galley."

I stopped in my tracks, "What?"

"Keep walking." Mom tugged my arm. I frowned and walked forward stiffly.

She said brightly, "I've never been on a DC-10 before, so I wasn't quite sure where the jumpseat was. So I just stood there until they all sat down, and I took the last one." She slapped her leg. "It was just like musical chairs.

"The other flight attendants must have known something was up. They kept asking me all these questions about where I was based and how long I had been working. I just stuck my nose in my magazine and pretended like I didn't hear them."

I stopped again. "You rode on the jumpseat? All the way from San Francisco? On my pass?"

What a Gal!

My mom had to backtrack a few steps and took my elbow to propel me forward. "Oh, Heather, you're too serious, relax! Everything worked out fine!"

Now I was getting really ticked. "And what were you going to do if there was an emergency and you needed to evacuate all those passengers?"

"Oh, I had that all figured out! I was going to hide in the bathroom until it was over!"

"MOM!"

Now she was mad at me. "Oh, chill out!" We reached the bathroom. "Here, hold my purse."

I put one hand out and looked the other way because I was so mad. She took her purse off her shoulder and hung it on my arm with two hands. I was not ready for how heavy the purse was, and it almost hit the floor.

She giggled, "Let's ride the subway. We'll be safe! I brought my gun!" She zipped into the bathroom with her index fingers in the air and her thumbs pulling the imaginary triggers. "Bang! Bang! Bang!"

I clutched her purse to my chest. I was frozen. I thought, *ARE YOU KIDDING? I am inside security with a gun! My mom rode on my pass . . . on the jumpseat . . . with a gun!*

She popped her head back out. "Oh Heather! Lighten up. It's heavy because I brought you five pounds of oranges from California! Don't worry. Be happy."

Chapter 20

THE OPPOSITE OF GLAMOROUS

In 1994, I was a pilot for American Eagle, a commuter airline. I was based in New York, and I made $12,600 per year. I ate ramen noodles. I stole orange juice and peanuts off the airplane. I took toilet paper from the hotels to bring back to my crash pad that I shared with 27 other broke pilots. Our schedules did not overlap. We were all gone more than half the month, so just like submariners with limited beds, 'hot racks' worked out unless our flights were canceled because of a massive snowstorm. In that case, we had to double up. Not very fun when you are the only chick in the group, but the house did have a lazy boy recliner, and I could sleep there.

This was not the glamorous career I had dreamed of.

The supply of pilots is very cyclical. It's a boom and bust. In 1994, no major airlines were hiring. To get an interview with a major airline (like United, American, Delta, or Northwest), you just about had to have a lunar landing and fly with the Blue Angels.

NEVER DULL!

Because I was at the bottom of the seniority list, I was bounced around from base to base and airplane to airplane. I was thinking, *God, my life sucks.*

Little did I know that He heard me. God was about to connect me with the right people.

I got bumped out of New York and based in Nashville on a smaller airplane. I rented a room from a very nice man named Bailey. He was older than my parents and from the hills of East Tennessee. He had a very thick southern accent, and when I met him for the first time, he said slowly, "So you fly, do ya'?"

"Yes, sir."

"That's funny." He flicked the ash off his cigarette and took a slow drag. He squinted his eyes. "I don't see no feather's on ya."

After that, he called me Feathers rather than Heather.

When I arrived in Nashville, I had no food in the house yet. Bailey offered me a fried baloney sandwich with an egg in the middle on white bread. I politely declined and decided to go to Applebee's for dinner.

I sat alone at the bar, stared into my chili, and wondered if I really wanted to continue being a pilot. I seriously considered changing careers. I thought, *It's like I am in an abusive relationship, but I can't leave because I love it so much.*

I looked so sad and pathetic. A guy came over to my table. He said, "Hey, are you OK?"

"Yeh, I'm fine."

He said, "You look familiar. Don't I know you?"

"Nope." I folded my napkin and signaled the waiter for the check.

"Oh, come on. What's your story?"

"Listen, buddy. There is no way possible that you know me. I just drove down here from New York. I don't have any food in my house and came here. I just want to eat my chili in peace."

"New York? Are you a singer? You came to Nashville to be discovered?"

"Nope. I fly for American Eagle."

"Oh! You're a stewardess."

I took a deep breath and sighed, "No, "I'm a pilot." I was so beaten down.

His eyes got big. He pulled back a chair, sat down, and slapped the table. "OK, forget the pickup line. I am THE minority recruiter for the entire Air National Guard. How many hours do you have?"

"3500."

"Wow." He got out his notebook and a pen. "We need minorities who can get through the training. What do you want to fly? I can hook you up with anything you want. F-15, F-16, you name it."

I knew I wanted to fly heavies. Single-seat was not for me. I knew I did not have the personality to be a fighter pilot.

He set me up with an interview with the Nashville Air National Guard the next day.

The interview went well, and I was excited about flying again. Thank you, God. He put me in the right place at the right time. My dad had been in the Army. He understood. I called him, and he was happy for me. My mom, not so much.

Before I signed on the dotted line, Mom wanted me to come to California so they could talk some sense into me. She could think of nothing worse than me joining the military and would barely speak to me. She and my dad cooked up some fictitious reason that I was needed to help my Dad on a vet call in Merced. She told Dad, " You will have lots of window time on the highway, and she won't be able to escape. Talk her out of it. Drive to Bakersfield if necessary. Heck, drive to South America if you need to."

The veterinary call never did materialize, and Dad and I had Mexican food in Merced. After talking with my dad and looking at the pros and cons, he said it was a good idea. He approved and said he would square it away with Mom.

Dad and I returned and told Mom together.

I said, "Don't worry, Mom. Everything will work out. It will all be okay."

She said, "Well, at least one good thing will come out of this, you'll wear a uniform. You're a fashion disaster."

I didn't say this out loud. I only thought it, *I'm a fashion disaster? Really? Maybe I inherited it from my dad.*

Let me tell you a little story about his proclivity for wigs and fake fingernails.

Every Halloween, John W. Jones, and his wife had a party at their house in Morro Bay. I went to Cal Poly in San Luis Obispo with my brother Brian and his future wife Debbie, and our entire family was invited.

RHONDA RUN AWAY AND THE
CHRISTMAS ORNAMENT

For the Halloween party, we dressed Dad up as a rodeo queen, complete with a blond wig, boobs, and a sash that said "Ronda Run Away.". My mild-mannered dad rode a stick horse into the party and did the queen wave as he galloped around the great room. He wore the buckle made of aluminum foil that Betty Steely made and then bragged to everyone how he won the buckle.

NEVER DULL!

He said something about *staying on for more than eight seconds.* I don't know what he said. I was plugging my ears and running away. I would need an emergency appointment with my therapist.

Mom was a Christmas ornament complete with tinsel and a tree skirt. Somehow, over the years, his outfit morphed into a Christmas ornament/rodeo queen, and they went to several parties. Several.

NOLAN AND GORDON
RASSMUSSEN

THE OPPOSITE OF GLAMOROUS

I know that he dressed up more than a few times because I have pictures of him with different shoes on, and his makeup and wig are different in each photo.

Years later, in 1994, I was the designated driver of my parents' motor home to Duane Martin's Christmas party. Jimmy and Mae Roddy, Don and Betty Steely, and Mom were getting Dad liquored up in the back of the motorhome while they dressed him up. They figured he needed to have a few belts to have the courage to go to the Christmas party.

I pulled over to a convenience store for some gas. It was quite busy, and I had to wait for a spot. A pack of ten motorcycle riders had their helmets off and were taking a smoke break. Mom and Betty had just finished gluing Dad's fake fingernails on with super glue. Jimmy ran in to get some more beer, and Dad followed him in because the toilet in the motor home didn't work. The toilet had its own story, but I won't go into that now.

Jimmy came out with a case of beer, followed by a very distressed six-foot-three Christmas ornament queen. His hands were glued to his underwear. He was panicked and yelling, "HELP! I need help!"

Jimmy looked over his shoulder, jumped in the motor home's back door, and yelled, "Drive, Heather! Drive!" I drove around the parking lot at three miles per hour while the gigantic ornament/rodeo queen did a slow-speed chase. He freed his hands and pounded on the door. Jimmy would not let him in. On the second lap around, he did the queen wave to the motorcycle group and sang, "Mamas, don't let your cowboys grow up to be babies."

We were late for the party because the Harley group wanted a picture with the rodeo queen on the back of their motorcycles. They offered to drive him to the party, but he declined because he felt, and I quote, "That would be too over the top."

Chapter 21

GULLIBLE

In 1997, I married Jack Schlichting. Yes, that's right. I still go by Sharp. I had been single too long, and no one could pronounce Captain Schlichting. Maybe if his last name was Hook or something fun, I would consider it.

I am lucky Jack tolerates me. As my dad said, *Who you marry is the most important decision you will ever make. It affects every facet of your life.*

I got the good end of the stick on that one. Jack, eh, maybe not so much. My little brother gave us a toast at our wedding. He said, "We welcome Jack to the family and express our condolan. . . sorry, our congratulations. We all hope and pray he has a happy life. When Jack dies and goes to Heaven, there will be two doors. There will be a long, long line of men waiting at the door labeled *Men who were dominated by their wives*. But Jack won't be in that line. He will be the only one standing in front of the door labeled, *Men who controlled their wives*. Saint Peter will approach Jack, welcome him to the kingdom of Heaven, and acknowledge all the hardships Jack endured on earth after he was married. Then Saint Peter will ask, But why are you standing in this line? Jack will reply, I don't know. Heather told me to stand here."

That's right. That was from my brother. On our wedding day! Poor little mistreated Heather.

A few months after the wedding, we visited Uncle Jimmy. We were looking at old photos and Jimmy told him the embarrassing stories about me.

Jack said, "I wish you would have told me this before."

"It's not too late."

"Yes it is. We're married. I lost the receipt. I can't return her."

"Yeah, and her parents won't take her back. They are too smart."

"Oh, don't give them too much credit. Remember that Christmas when Mom thought she fooled you?"

Jimmy looked puzzled.

"We were looking at photo albums just like we are now. Mom thought you did not know about her facelift. She was so mad at me!'

"What? What are you talking about?"

"You don't remember? I looked at a photo and asked, "Who's that lady?" Mom jabbed me in the ribs and told me to shut up. She hissed in my ear, "That's me! Jimmy doesn't know."

"What!" He was still baffled, and nothing was registering.

"Mom slammed the photo books closed and took them to the back room. I followed her in and said, 'Mom! Your own daughter can't recognize you, and you don't think your brother is going to notice!' She slammed the door, and that was the end of our little trip down memory lane. You don't remember that?"

"I remember you were on the naughty list. What are you saying about a facelift?"

"Oh, come on!" I said, "Seriously? You don't know? She was very proud of it, she told everybody."

"What!" He sat back heavily and crossed his arms over his chest. He stared out the window. I could see his brain churning, trying to process this. He opened his mouth a few times to say something, but no words would come out each time he tried to speak.

Finally, he said, "I wondered why she looked so good and the rest of us looked so bad."

I laughed, "I asked her once about it, and she told me it was like having a car. She said if you had a car, you would take it in for maintenance."

My husband is from the Midwest. He laughed, "You would have the oil changed. You wouldn't take it in for a major rebuild!"

I grinned, "That might be true in the Midwest, but not in California."

Jimmy asked, "What all did she have done?"

"Oh . . . let me think, the list is long . . . she had her boobs, her teeth, her chin, her eyes, her nose, her butt. She had a skin peel once and looked like a pumpkin."

Jimmy said, "I can't believe it."

I said, "Jimmy, don't look so shocked. Everybody knew."

"She never told me!"

"She probably thought you were being polite by never mentioning it to her."

"But I've never been polite!"

He looked out the window and was silent for a while. "I don't get it. Why didn't she get three boobs, then?" He put his hands out like he was ready for a dance partner. "You know?" He squeezed his right hand like testing a melon. "One in the back . . . for dancin'?"

In 2001, Ted and Barb Ryan invited Mom and Dad to the Margarita Ride in Sonoita, Arizona. Ted is a team roper and goes on the RV ride with Dad. He supplied the four horses, and they borrowed a motorhome.

Ted came from Arizona to Mom and Dad's 50th Anniversary party.

50TH ANNIVERSARY
2014

GULLIBLE

Ted tells the story:

I have known them for years, we hit it off right away. He came over our house to rope with us in Arizona and my horse about bucked him off. I said, well gee, you got to warm him up a little bit.

Nolan and Marion came over to many rides with us. And we came over one time to the Margarita ride in Sonoita, Arizona. We had a motor home and we were sitting there having a good time and had a great ride. I supplied the four horses. They just flew over and came to Arizona and we had a great time on the trail ride. We came home and gave the motor home back to the people that I borrowed it from and it blew up the next week.

I called Nolan, I say, guess what, Nolan? The motor home blew up! Thank God it didn't blow up while we were there." It turned out to be a propane leak that caused the explosion, melted the tires, and left behind a burning frame of the motor home.

Nolan said, how 'bout that? You know, I was going to call you. I lost a watch in that motor home.

I said, what kind of a watch was it?

I am pretty sure it was a Rolex.

I said, well, I'll turn it into insurance!

Barb and I went to Mexico for vacation the next week and bought a Rolex on the beach for 20 bucks. The next time we saw Nolan, I said, Nolan! The claim came in. We got your watch!

Holy cow. Nolan said, I always wanted a Rolex. (laughter)

The watch worked for about 30 days, and then it crapped out. Nolan dropped it off at the local jeweler to get it fixed. When he filled out the paperwork, he wrote down that it was insured for $5,000. A few days went by, and the jeweler called him back and said, I don't know how to tell you, but this watch is a fake. We got you on that one, Nolan!

Dad told me about a trip he and Mom took with other couples from the RV ride in 2007. They went to Italy and had an absolutely fantastic time. Before returning to the States, Mom and Dad split off to see the countryside.

Dad said, "I knew I was in capable hands with Mom. There was no telling what she would have in store. She is so worldly, and there is always something exciting."

They went to a secluded little spa in the hills of Tuscany. The men went in on one side and the women on the other. The hostess showed Dad around and used sign language because she spoke no English. She pointed out the hot springs, steam room, shower room, and massage room. He would bow deeply and smile at each location to show he understood. She handed him a towel, some flip-flops, and a black thing made out of satin with elastic. He told me it looked like the eye mask they had on the flight over. She gestured for him to lie face up on the table. He put his fingers together in prayer and bowed deeply.

"Dad, you're in Italy, not Japan!"

"I know! But it was so tranquil. I was transported."

"Awww, my little country bumpkin."

He said, "Just wait. It gets worse."

Since only men were on his side, he went in the hot springs and the steam bath in the buff. He took a shower and then went into the massage room. He hung up the towel, kicked off his flip-flops, and looked at the black satin thing. He tried to make sense of it and thought, *I have never been to a spa as nice as this. We are overseas. There will probably be ultraviolet light.*

He struggled with the satiny thing and could not make it fit properly over his eyes. There was a soft knock at the door. He quickly laid face up on the table. He had it half on his head. He looked like a pirate wearing an eye patch.

The young massage therapist opened the door and shrieked when she saw him lying there in all his glory, with the G-string around his head.

She slammed the door and ran away. A much older, hefty woman replaced her. Dad said, "Helga came in, snatched the thing off my head, and threw a towel at my nuts!"

I laughed at my poor dad.

He cried, "She gripped my head with her very large hands and flipped me over on my stomach. She pummeled me with such force that I had bruises the next day."

I was cracking up.

GULLIBLE

Dad wailed, "The abuse lasted for ninety minutes! Now I can't go back to Europe because I am on the lamb as a sexual deviant."

I had missed Mom's 65th birthday and wanted to surprise her. I was a pilot for Delta Air Lines and had a layover in California. I knew she would be at the all-girl Dos Cheekas trail ride in Red Bluff. Many of the ladies' husbands go on the RV ride and Lori McCarthy thought the wives should have their own ride.

It sounds like Dos Chicas, Spanish for "two girls," but it is spelled with a K. Get it, Dos Cheekas—two cheeks?

These girls are naughty. R-rated doesn't even come close. Their motto was, *What happens at the ranch, stays at the ranch.* The board of directors spent all year thinking up crazy games, contests, and skits. There was a lot of depravity, a lot of laughter, and a lot of booze.

I had been on this trail ride with my mom in the past, and it was a ball.

GULLIBLE

After I landed in Sacramento, I borrowed a reflective vest from the ground crew and rented a car. In my suitcase, I brought a disguise. I had my husband's khaki pants, his khaki shirt, a baseball cap, a wig, sunglasses, gloves, a walking cane, and a clipboard. I printed out two large signs that said "Compliance Officer" and "Vehicle for Official Use Only," complete with the City of Red Bluff seal. I even made myself a name tag, "Ben Dover." Get it? Bend over.

TEHAMA COUNTY COMPLIANCE
OFFICER

GULLIBLE

My goal was to time my arrival perfectly. I knew they would just be finishing up riding and were about to start drinking the Dos Cheekas punch. It had all the ingredients of a Long Island Iced Tea in a five-gallon beverage cooler. Accurately labeled with duct tape and a marker: "Barrel of Fun." On a hot day, that cooler gets emptied pretty fast. I knew the group would be feeling no pain by the time I arrived.

DOS CHEEKAS PUNCH

GULLIBLE

I drove up Highway 5 to Red Bluff and pulled off three miles from the ranch to tape the signs to the car doors and don my disguise. I brought a few pillows off the airplane to stuff under my shirt to create a beer belly. I practiced walking around and leaning on my cane with what I hoped was a believable limp.

A flatbed Ford driven by an old-timer slowed down as it drove by. I tipped my hat and waved. He went past me, stopped, and started to reverse. I squealed, "Holy Crap!" And hobbled as fast as I could back to my car.

He stopped in front of my car. "Need any help?"

I practiced my graveling voice and an accent. "Nope, no, I thank ye tho'. I was just about to relieve myself when you came along."

"All right then." He was suspicious but nodded. "Carry on." He slowly pulled away.

"Much obliged." I started coughing into my red handkerchief because I was cracking myself up.

I collected myself and got in the car. I drove to the ranch, turned down the long lane, and parked near the arena. But not too close. I didn't want to give away my real identity yet. I was an old man, after all. I did my best Tim Conway impression and made a big production getting out of the car. I wanted to give them time to read the sign on my door.

I limped toward the arena and yelled, "Who's in charge here?" I knew Lori McCarthy's sister Merilee would be the first one I encountered. She did not ride because of her hips and was dubbed Camp Security. She wore a huge foam blue hat, black rubber boots, a six-shooter toy gun, and a belt of ammunition. In the belt . . . she had jello shots.

She had already had a few belts of that Dos Cheekas punch and I wasn't prepared for how aggressive she would be.

MERILEE EVASOVIC IS CAMP
SECURITY

She marched over to me and was irate. She was screaming that this was private property and ordered me to leave. I was worried she was getting too close and would see that I was in costume. I raised my cane like I was going to hit her, "Back off, you wild filly!"

The cowgirls heard the commotion, and more reinforcements arrived.

Now I was surrounded by ten drunk ladies who were all yelling at me. I banged my clipboard with my cane and told them I had to see their Coggins papers and a permit for a gathering; if not, I would haul them all into the Tehama County Jail. This lasted only a short while until someone figured out I was an imposter.

That someone, I might add, was sober and recognized me. I whispered to her, "Where's my mom?" She pointed down the hill to my mom's horse trailer.

"She's unsaddling her horse. Go down there and surprise her." The sober one called for a huddle, she told them who I was, and they made a plan.

I got in my car and drove down to Mom's trailer. She was far enough away and completely unaware of the melee that had just occurred near the arena. I shuffled over to her trailer, consulted my clipboard, and shouted, "Which of you here is Marian Sharp?"

Mom stopped brushing and was sizing up the situation. She saw the other ladies coming down the road from the arena. The posse was yelling at me. I was afraid there might be a hanging.

She demanded, "Who the hell are you?"

BEN DOVER IN PURSUIT OF MARIAN (FAR LEFT)

"I am an officer of the law!"

Mom's confidence was fortified by the group of girls coming to her rescue. She was snobby when she informed me, "This is private property. You have no right to be here."

I coughed into my handkerchief to cover up my laughing. "Oh, I see! You're familiar with the warrant process, then?"

Mom wasn't even drunk yet. But she got her Irish up and became enraged. "What!"

"Ah-ha! This isn't your first rodeo, then? You have been arrested before?"

"What!"

I looked at my clipboard, "Marian Sharp, you are under arrest and being extricated back to Contra Costa County to face charges for the Pyramid Ponzi scheme." It was liberating to yell at the top of my lungs at my mom—something I was never allowed to do before. I let 'er rip.

"What!"

I just knew she would figure out this was a joke, so I kept feeding her information, hoping she would figure out who I was.

"And you were seen naked at the airport in Washington, DC."

"What!"

"You're not very smart, are you? You keep saying the same word."

"What!"

"And there you go again." I feared my voice was giving me away. "You are facing child abuse charges! What about all those terrible, horrible things you did to your daughter Heather!"

She didn't even hear me. Her face was red, and she was yelling obscenities at me along with the rest of the crowd.

I waved my cane wildly and shouted, "Don't get sassy with me, young lady!"

Now they were chanting. I can't remember exactly what it was, but something like "Death! Death!" They were crazed.

I yelled out to the group, "Seize her!" Then the crowd turned on her. One woman was a police officer in real life. Katherine Comesana put Mom's hands behind her and put her in the back of my car just like she was really being arrested. Katherine opened the door with one hand, knocked off Mom's cowboy hat, and guided her into the car so Mom would not hit her head. Now the ladies were swarming around the car and banging on the hood.

I took my hat and wig off. I said, "This is so much better than I could have imagined. It's a dream come true." Now Mom was mad at all of them and pounded the window to get out. I pushed the ladies out of the way and opened the passenger door. I stuck my head in and said to her in the backseat, "Happy birthday, Mom!" She was stunned for a moment and then roared with laughter.

I could tell by the look on her face and the way she crossed her legs that we were only moments from a disaster.

"Oh no! Don't you dare pee in my car Mom!" I screamed to the ladies, "Red alert! Red alert. Get her out!"

The drunk ladies opened the back door and were trying to get her out. Mom had lost all muscle control. When they yanked on her arm to pull her out, the ladies fell to the ground, and Mom fell on top of them. She peed her pants.

That's all it took. I collapsed to the ground and peed my pants too.

Chapter 22

Know What's Important

In 2004, they sold their property on Tassajara Road to a developer and moved to Steamboat Springs, Colorado.

MARIAN AND NOLAN BEFORE LEAVING
FOR STEAMBOAT SPRINGS - 2004

Never Dull!

When they moved to Colorado, the cashier at Ace Hardware said to Dad, "That's odd. Most people, when they retire, move away from the snow, not to it." By 2011, the snow got to be too much for them.

Right after they moved back to California, Mom started to lose vision in her right eye. The doctor found a tumor the size of an orange growing on her optic nerve. John Muir Hospital successfully removed a benign meningioma. We were all so thankful to God that it was not cancerous.

She told her brothers and sister that she had had brain surgery. One of them asked, "So when they opened up your head, did they find anything in there?"

She just laughed.

Actually, Mom was not the first one that had brain surgery. Mom is ultra-competitive and doesn't want to be left out. I was first.

I had brain surgery in 2010 but that is a whole other story. I should have been dead. It is a miracle I am still here. In 2021, I medically retired from flying.

Now I do public speaking about how important faith and attitude are to our everyday lives. I thank God every day and attribute my recovery to the lessons I learned from my parents.

KNOW WHAT IS IMPORTANT

75 AND 80 YEARS OLD AND STILL
LAUGHING - 2015

Dad died in 2018 after a long battle with Parkinson's. The following is a transcription from Dad's Celebration of Life. My son, Ryan speaks first, and then my brother, Brian.

Ryan

We really did look up to Nolan, and we always wanted to be as much like him as we could. And I always tried to do that by beating him in chess. Every time I went to Grandma and Grandpa's, I would pull out the chess board. I'd say, 'Grandpa, let's play!' And every time, I got my butt kicked. Pretty badly!

But I had a plan. It was about two years ago, and he was in the care center. It was very hard for him to talk at this time, and he was bedridden. And I'm like, 'I've got you now. Let's play chess!'

And so, I pulled out the chess board, and we started playing. And then I was looking at the board, and I'm like, I'm losing. And then, a few turns later, I realize I'm really losing.

PLAYING CHESS

There was not even a chance that I was going to win this game. And I look over at him, and he's just sitting there smiling in his bed as he moves his pieces forward. And I'm like, this guy really is a genius. Because even at the end of his life, he was still really smart and a really great guy and a man of character, as Grant was saying.

And so I did try to pull a fast one on him, but he ended up winning that game and then the next game and the game after that. And it still amazes me. That's what really sticks in my head about Grandpa.

What really stuck in my head was that I can't think of a time when Grandpa would tell me a story about him. I've heard hundreds of stories of the Roddys. I've heard about the time that Brian shot his foot. I've heard about all these stories, but I can't remember a time when he would sit down with me and tell me, I did THIS when I was a kid. I did THAT when I was a kid. And what I really take away from that was that Nolan really was a humble man.

RYAN AND GRANDPA 2017

He had so much to brag about again, one year NHS and being incredibly popular. Still, he never bragged, and he always wanted to give credit to others, credit to God, and credit to everyone who deserves it. And that sticks in my head is he doesn't want the attention on himself. He just wants to live life to the best that he can and help others along when he can.

Brian

My dad was a great guy, and when I was younger, I used to look at my mom and say, boy, my dad really married well. She's pretty. She's funny. She's the life of the party. I'm not taking anything away from my mom. As I got older, I realized she married pretty well, too. I cannot recall anybody ever saying anything bad about my dad, ever. He always had a kind word. Never tried to cheat anybody. Never tried to take advantage or make someone look bad. He

BRIAN AND NOLAN AT A BRANDING

was the hardest worker I've ever seen. He was optimistic, almost to a fault.

And I should mention, you see these pictures? The horses that he is on are not our best horses. Heather and I always got the best horses. He would get on the colt, and Heather and I would have the trained horses. Very unselfish.

There's a Bible verse I want to read from First Corinthians. It talks about love.

This is one thing I've told my kids; one way to test yourself is to put your name in this verse and see how you're doing. I'm going to do that for my dad.

Nolan is patient. Nolan is kind. He does not envy. He does not boast. He is not proud. He does not dishonor others. He is not self-seeking. He is not easily angered. He keeps no record of wrongs. Nolan does not delight in evil but rejoices with the truth. He always protects, always trusts, always hopes, and always perseveres. Nolan never fails.

That describes my dad perfectly.

Beginning in 2015, my dad's caregiver was Romeo. He is a wonderful man who immigrated from the Philippines.

Very soon after my dad died, Romeo's lease was up, and he needed to find another place to live. I asked him, "Hey, can you live with my mom?"

ROMEO, MARIAN, AND CJAY - 2018

KNOW WHAT IS IMPORTANT

The rumor around her neighborhood was *Nolan has been dead less than a week, and Marian had already moved a man in!*

Romeo rented a room from my mom for a few years and saw other clients until Mom needed more care, and then he became her full-time caregiver. My brother and I cannot say enough about how wonderful he was to our parents. His son, CJay, and daughter-in-law, Dyan, also cared for Mom. They are like family; we are so blessed to have them in our lives.

After Dad died, my mom was still pretty spry but slowing down, and in 2022 her balance got really bad, and her right arm became paralyzed. She had the brain tumor removed in 2011, but I wondered if it was growing back and causing neurological problems. Her attitude was always very good, and she was easy to care for.

Six months before she died, I had this bright idea to take Mom and her best friend Leslie to the botanical gardens and then have lunch: Leslie, the same one from the peeing our pants in the elevator story. We planned to enjoy the day and relive all the old times.

Mom was in a wheelchair at the time. I am a good pilot but not a very good driver. Most of the paths in the botanical gardens were paved, but there was a gravel shortcut with several potholes.

Typical of our whole life together, Mom talked me into taking the shortcut. The front wheel hit a pothole, and in slow motion, Mom fell out of the wheelchair and tumbled to the ground like a rag doll. On her way down, she was screaming, "Elder abuse! Elder abuse!" She lay there on the gravel and started laughing. She was laughing so hard that she wound up peeing her pants.

Leslie said, "Oh no! Not again!"

Mom crying with laughter, "Just let me die right here. There are lots of flowers. Just dig a hole."

Leslie said, "No! We haven't had lunch yet."

LESLIE, MARIAN AND HEATHER - 2022

KNOW WHAT IS IMPORTANT

Because I was retired, I was with Mom for the last few weeks of her life. So, a bad thing (my accidents) resulted in a good thing, being with Mom.

The Bible tells us in Romans 8:28:

> And we know that in all things, God works for the good of those who love him, who have been called according to his purpose.

I posted updates to Facebook and read her all of the good wishes and prayers everyone sent. I can assure you she felt the love from all of you.

In her last days, we looked at 82 years of photos. She told me many of these stories you just read. She really did have an extraordinary life. I told her, "I'm going to write a book."

She shrugged and dismissed my idea. "Go ahead; no one will believe it anyway. They all know how shy and conservative I am. I was boring."

"Ya, right."

The hospice nurse came right then and wanted to give Mom a suppository for comfort. She shrugged her shoulders. "Eh, I don't think I need it. I've never been in any pain." The fact that she was never in any pain is amazing to me. I saw the X-rays of her neck. It was bone on bone. Her hands were misshapen due to arthritis. I asked her about her hands and she held them up, "You mean these claws? I look like a lobster." She had an incredibly high pain tolerance. I think it was mind over matter. She didn't let thing anything bother her.

From when she was 19 and her ponytail was cut off and handed to her; to when the UPS man found her naked while hanging upside down, to brain surgery and laughing when she was asked if the surgeon actually found a brain in her head.

She laughed it off and kept moving forward. Now her body was letting her down, and she was ready to move forward.

We talked about how when she gets to Heaven, she will get a new body. I said, "Except you Mom! You have great hair. You will probably keep that hair. But the rest of your body will be new."

The Hospice nurse saw all the photos scattered across her bed and asked about them. I told her some stories, and she was blown away.

Mom told her, "Don't believe anything Heather says. She is full of shit!"

"Mom! It has been four days since you pooped. You are full of shit!"

KNOW WHAT IS IMPORTANT

The nurse asked her, "So, are they true? Or is she making all this up?"

Mom feigned embarrassment, but you could see the pride coming through, "I am sad to say, they're all true."

The nurse left, and the priest came in to give her the last rites. Mom rolled over on her side and put her hands under her cheek. She closed her eyes. I kissed her head and sat down.

After he left, She rolled back over, "How long is this going to take?"

"So typical. You are always in a hurry. I don't know, Mom. You're a pretty tough cookie." She was with us for four more days.

I was with her when she took her last breath and went to be with Dad. She was there when I came into this world, and I was blessed to be with her when she went out.

One of the last things she said was how proud she was of her kids and grandkids and how much she loved her friends and family. She wanted me to tell everyone how much they meant to her and how lucky she was to have them in her life. She told Romeo what a wonderful person he is and how much she appreciates everything he's done for her. And Nolan.

She said a prayer to God. Then she said she was getting a little tired and would take a nap. I played Irish music and tucked her in. She closed her eyes.

Then she opened one eye, pointed her finger, and said, "Oh, and one more thing. I love Nolan."

THE COWBOY'S PRAYER

by Donna McSpadden

Our gracious and heavenly Father, we pause in the midst of this festive occasion, mindful of the many blessings you have bestowed upon us.

As cowboys, Lord, we don't ask for any special favors. We ask only that you will let us compete in this arena as in the arena of life.

We don't ask that we never break a barrier, draw around a chute-fighting horse, or draw a steer that just won't lay. We don't even ask for all daylight runs.

We only ask that you help us to compete in life as honest as the horses we ride and in a manner as clean and pure as the wind that blows across this great land of ours.

Help us, Lord, to live our lives in such a manner that when we make that last inevitable ride to the country up there, where the grass grows lush, green, and stirrup high, and the water runs cool, clear, and deep, that you, as our last Judge, will tell us that our entry fees are paid.

Amen.

Heather Sharp(1966) married Jack Schlichting in 1997. They have two boys, Grant (1999) and Ryan (2002) Schlichting

RYAN 20, HEATHER, JACK, GRANT 23 - 2022

Brian Sharp (1968) married Debbie Loesche in 1995 they have five children. Austin (1999), Megan (2002), Brandon and Brianna (2005), and Maya (2006)

BRANDON 17, BRIANNA 17, DEBBIE, MAYA 16, BRIAN, AUSTIN 23, MEGAN 20 - 2023

THANK YOU

Jacqueline Kyle for the cover.

Janan Smith, Rita Bakken, and Heidi "Eagle Eye" Huffman for proofreading.

Travsonic for editing the audiobook.

And my husband, Jack for putting up with me. He vowed for better or worse. Two near death accidents and all the challenges we have faced make me thankful that I have a such a wonderful partner to travel this rocky road with. I love you.

Coming soon by Heather Sharp

GROUNDED

Cannon Falls, Minnesota - October 31, 2010

Over the years, our horses chewed the bark off the trees in their pasture. For months I complained, "Jack, we gotta knock down those dead trees. When we least expect it, they are going to fall the fence and the horses are going to get loose and get hit on the highway."

This morning he said, "Today you get your wish. Come outside and help."

So far he had knocked down six trees with our skid steer. I said, "This looks great. Totally transformed. Incredible how fast things can change." At four o'clock, Jack drove out of the pasture. I said, "Where are you going?"

"I'm putting it away so we can take the boys trick-or-treating."

"Oh, come on. We have plenty of time; let's do one more." That statement is so typical. I always want to squeeze in one more thing.

He said, "It's a farm. The work is never done. Why do we have to jam-pack everything into one day?"

I am so hard-headed. I crossed my arms and glared. "I have to fly a four-day tomorrow. Let's do it now." He figured it was faster to go along rather than argue with me.

He turned the skid steer around and approached the next tree. It was bent at a weird angle. It turns out the top was dead but not the roots. He later referred to it as a *widow maker* and it almost was. I stood beside the skid steer with our eight-year-old son Ryan on my left. When Jack pushed on the tree, the top snapped. A branch eight inches around fell on my head and then broke over my head.

I collapsed.

Jack did not see the tree fall, but heard Ryan's shrieking over the roar of the skid steer. Ryan was only inches away from me. If the tree landed on him, he would have been dead. Ryan ran inside and screamed at eleven-year-old Grant to call 911.

Because we live in a small town, the same paramedic from my first accident got the call. She heard the address and could not believe it. She arrived within minutes and saw me lying on the ground with a trickle of blood coming out of my nose and thought *this time she's dead for sure.*

I gasped.

She yelled to her partner, "Helicopter!"

The same helicopter that came and got me the first time came and airlifted me again, not the same pilot but the same helicopter.

Jack sped down the highway to the Emergency Room at the Mayo Clinic. Things happened so fast back there, he really didn't know what all happened. While waiting in line gripped his keys so tight his knuckles turned white. He glanced at the crowded waiting lounge. People were talking on their cells in hushed voices. A man angrily punched the buttons on the vending machine and then put his forehead on the glass and cried in frustration.

Jack shut his eyes and turned away. It was too painful to watch. Two years ago that was him. Waiting and wondering. Angry to be so powerless. Hungry for any news, but scared of what he might be told.

While he stood in line, he texted Heather's best friend, another pilot: H hurt. In ER, text num 4 chief pilot 2 me, need 2 call in sic 4 H.

The receptionist said, "May I help you?"

"My wife, Heather Sharp, came here by helicopter?"

She consulted a clipboard. "Follow me, please."

"Thanks for taking me to her. Two years ago, I had to sit in that waiting room for hours." He followed her and felt relieved. Last time, he was scared out of his mind, but she got back to work and healed up one hundred percent. As they walked down a corridor, he said, "It is hard not to jump to the worst possible conclusion."

She barely nodded and opened the door to a small room with dim lighting and stuffed chairs. She gestured for him to take a seat, "The doctor will be right with you," And gently closed the door.

Jack looked at the boxes of Kleenex on every coffee table and his heart stopped. "Uh-oh. This can't be good."

Two minutes later, a man dressed in scrubs came in and introduced himself, but all Jack heard was, "I'll be the doctor doing the brain surgery on your wife. We are going to remove part of her skull to cauterize the bleeding on her brain. She has twelve fractures in her back and a collapsed lung. Surgery will begin immediately."

Jack nodded. Unable to speak.

"I wanted to tell you personally that we are doing everything we possibly can. But you should prepare yourself. She might die."

The surgeon said more words that Jack did not hear and left Jack alone.

Jack fell to his knees and prayed.

To be notified when Grounded is released, please join the mailing list at www.heathersharp.com.

One last thing . . . .

To the reader,

Could I ask a big favor? Could you leave a review on Amazon? Historically, only 10% of people will not take the time to do it, but I know I can count on you.

Search **Books** for Never Dull!

Otherwise, if you do a global search, you will come up with a metal polish. After having two brain injuries, I have heard all the jokes about being hardheaded, but metal polish is taking it a bit too far, don't you think?

If you laughed when you read it, go to your Amazon account or use this QR code and there is a white button about halfway down on the left.

If you hated it . . . . Well . . . just put it under a table leg so it doesn't wobble, and forget I ever said this. 😉

All the best,

Heather